MW00465564

Spiritual Warfare Ministries Presents:

THE
WITCHCRAFT
OF
PROFANITY

The Truth About Demons and Profanity

Kenneth Scott

Scriptures in this publication are taken from the King James version of the Bible or paraphrased by the author.

Print 5b

The Witchcraft of Profanity

Spiritual Warfare Ministries
Attention: Kenneth Scott
P.O. Box 2024
Birmingham, Alabama 35201-2024

(205) 853-9509

Contents

Let no corrupt communication proceed out of your mouth, but that which is good to the use of edifying, that it may minister grace unto the hearers.
Ephesians 4:29

INTRODUCTION

In the book of Revelations, chapter 2, Jesus gave a stern rebuke to the church of Pergamos for practicing the *Doctrine of Balaam*. The Doctrine of Balaam consists of the two things that Balak attempted to get Balaam to do to God's people. First, Balak enticed Balaam to curse God's people by offering him a substantial amount of money. After that didn't work, Balak further enticed Balaam with even more money to teach him how to destroy them.

Tempted by the enormous amount of money which Balak offered, Balaam taught Balak how to lure and seduce God's people to commit idolatry and get involved in witchcraft. This led to many of them being destroyed.

In this book we will lean how we have (through both the ignorance of our words and the use of profanity) also practiced this demonic doctrine. We will learn that profanity is not just empty, vain words, but words that bring us into the darkness of witchcraft. We will also explore many of these profane words, their meaning, and their demonic involvement.

As you learn what is going on in the spiritual realm when you use profanity, it is my prayer that you will turn your heart away from it and stop the use of profanity. Once you do this, it will cut off Satan's access to your life, remove demonic hindrances, and put you in a position to receive the blessings of the Lord upon your life.

Chapter 1

THE DOCTRINE OF BALAAM AND WITCHCRAFT

THE DOCTRINE OF BALAAM

*And to the angel of the church in Pergamos write;
These things saith he which hath the sharp sword
with two edges; I know thy works and where thou
dwellest, even where Satan's seat is: and thou hold-
est fast my name, and hast not denied my faith, even
in those days wherein Antipas was my faithful mar-
tyr, who was slain among you, where Satan dwel-
leth. But I have a few things against thee, **because
thou hast there them that hold the <u>doctrine of
Balaam</u>**, who taught Balak to cast a stumblingblock
before the children of Israel, to eat things sacrificed
unto idols, and to commit fornication.*

Rev 2:12-13

In Revelations chapter 2, Jesus speaks to the seven
churches of Asia. In the above passage He speaks specifically to the church of Pergamos. He begins by first
commending them for their spiritual accomplishments.
But while commending them for these things, He also
rebukes them for holding fast to the *Doctrine of Balaam*.
To find how this doctrine (the doctrine of Balaam) relates to the subject of cursing and profanity, you must
go back to find who Balaam was and what he did.

Balaam and Balak

Balaam was an Old Testament prophet (Num. 22-24). God had just brought the children of Israel out of Egyptian bondage and they were encamped outside Moab. The king of the Moabites was a king by the name of Balak. Balak didn't know Israel's intentions and thought perhaps they would plunder their land on the way through it, or worse, destroy them and take their land.

Balak had heard about the mighty miracles that God used to deliver the Israelites from Egypt. Egypt at that time was the military world power. Balak knew that if God was with them to defeat Egypt, that his small nation would be powerless against the Israelites and their God. So, since a military campaign against them would have been impossible, he sought for another course of action.

Since God was with them supernaturally, he figured that the only way he could defeat them was to fight against them supernaturally. Balak knew of a prophet who lived in his land by the name of Balaam. He had heard that God's hand and favor was upon Balaam to such a degree, that whomever he would bless (with the words of his mouth) would supernaturally receive the blessings and favor of God; and, on the contrary, whomever he cursed would be cursed. So instead of attempting to wage an impossible war against them, he planed to get supernatural help to fight against them through this prophet Balaam.

Come now therefore, I pray thee, curse me this people; for they are too mighty for me: peradventure I shall prevail, that we may smite them, and that I may drive them out of the land: for I wot [know] that he whom thou blessest is blessed, and he whom thou cursest is cursed. (Num 22:6)

The above passage entails the message that Balak sent to Balaam. He wanted Balaam to curse the people of God with his mouth — hoping that God would honor Balaam's words and destroy them. To entice Balaam to do this, he sent messengers loaded with all kinds of costly jewels, gold and riches for him. They eventually arrived to Balaam and made the request on behalf of Balak. Balaam knew this request was wrong and ungodly, but because of the enticement of Balak's money, he entertains the guests of Balak and tells them to wait while he asks God. During the night Balaam sought God for the answer (which he already knew). The following is the answer in which God gave to Balaam.

And God said unto Balaam, thou shalt not go with them; thou shalt not curse the people: for they are blessed. (Num 22:12)

Balaam arose in the morning and gave the message to Balak's messengers to take back to him. But Balak was determined to persuade Balaam to curse them because he knew that this was his only way to defeat them. So he sent the messengers back to Balaam again. This time he sent them with many times the wealth and riches he originally sent the first time.

The messengers once again approached Balaam with Balak's request to curse the people. Even though Balaam knew it was wrong for him to curse them in the first place, and even though God had already given him the answer telling him not to curse them, Balaam continued and asked God if he could do it. Again, God's answer was the same.

Balak tried relentlessly to get Balaam to curse God's people. But although Balak could not get Balaam to curse them (in this part of the story), the story does not end there. To get the conclusion of the story, you have to go back to our original passage in Revelations:

> *But I have a few things against thee, because thou hast there them that hold the <u>doctrine of Balaam</u>, who taught Balak to cast a stumblingblock; who taught Balak to cast a stumblingblock before the children of Israel, to eat things sacrificed unto idols, and to commit fornication.* (Rev 2:12-13)

This passage in Revelations brings out something Balaam did that the book of Numbers doesn't show. It shows us the end result of Balaam's treachery. Because Balaam was so enticed by the riches Balak offered, even though he couldn't curse the people of God with his mouth, he taught Balak how to destroy them.

He told Balak to send their Moabite women in the camp to entice them to sin. Balak sent these women into the Israelite camp and they enticed the men of the camp to commit sexual immorality and perversions. God had strictly forbade the Israelites from marrying or joining (having sex) with the heathen women of these nations.

In spite of God's strict warnings, they brought these women in the camp and began to marry and intermingle (have sex) with them. These Moabite women not only led them into sexual immorality and perversions, they also lured the men of Israel to commit idolatry and practice witchcraft.

> *And Israel abode in Shittim, and the people began to commit whoredom with the daughters of Moab. And they called [lured] the people unto the sacrifices of their gods: and the people did eat, and bowed down to their gods. And Israel joined himself unto Baalpeor: and the anger of the LORD was kindled against Israel.* (Num 25:1-3)

In addition to Israel's sexual abominations, these Moabite women lured the Israelites into doing things that was detestable to the Living God. The Israelites began eating foods that were strictly forbidden by God (foods that had been sacrificed to the Moabite gods). They caused them to bow down and worship their gods. They even caused the Israelites to worship the Moabite god, Baalpeor, and to observe its occult practices. These practices included debase sexual deviances, worshiping the dead, and various forms of witchcraft.

Because of Israel's defiance to God and His sacred commandments, God's anger was kindled against them. Because of Israel's sin and blatant disobedience, God sent a plague among them that killed twenty-four thousand Israelites. After they began suffering and dying, the people of Israel began to repent of their sins. They got rid of the Moabite women that were causing them to commit sexual immorality, they got rid of the Moabite idols, stopped their idol worship and practices, stopped their occult and witchcraft practices, and once again turned their hearts to the Living God. Eventually God had mercy upon them and stopped the plague. God then had Moses and the Israelites to wage war against the Moabites, and they destroyed Balak and the Moabites.

The Doctrine of Balaam Put Simple

This incident in Israelite history became known as the Doctrine of Balaam. The Doctrine of Balaam is what Balak attempted to do to Israel using the prophet Balaam. First, he tried to entice Balaam through money to put a curse on them. After this did not work, he enticed Balaam to show him how to destroy them. Because of the money, Balaam showed Balak how to get them to destroy themselves through luring them into sexual perversions, idolatry, occult practices, and the practice of witchcraft.

Put short, the Doctrine of Balaam is two-fold: First, it's when a Christian curses someone with their mouth (words they speak). Secondly, it's when a Christian (intentionally or unintentionally) get involved in witchcraft, and through it cause hindrances, physical or spiritual harm, or cause evil spirits to come in or upon their lives or the lives of others.

In this book we are going to look at the two spectrums of the Doctrine of Balaam. First, we are going to look at how a Christian can (through negative words) place a curse on their lives and the lives of others. Next, we will look at how Christians (through the ignorance of using profanity) get involved in witchcraft, and through it evoke evil and demonic spirits.

SPEAKING SPIRITS

In our previous topic we discovered that there are two different aspects of the Doctrine of Balaam. The first aspect of the Doctrine of Balaam is what Balak attempted to get Balaam to do in the beginning—curse God's people.

Let me begin by first stating that there is a difference between cursing and profanity. Cursing is simply any lies, negative words, statements, or comments we make with our mouths regarding other people. Profanity is when we use vile, profane words of expression regarding someone. In this first section we are going to take a look at the first one—cursing.

Do We Have the Power to Place
A Curse on Someone?

To answer the question of whether or not we have the power to curse someone, we have to go all the way back to the beginning.

* **Note:** Before I get into this subject, I want to encourage you to be patient and read this entire topic. I know that you are probably anxious to get to the main focus on profanity, but it is very important that you understand this subject first. So please be patient, and in chapter two we will pick up on the topic of profanity and the understanding of our involvement with demons when we use profanity.

The Breath of Life — Speaking Spirits

In the book of Genesis God created all the animals and living creatures of the earth with the power of His Word. God spoke and said, *"Let there be..."* and it was. But when God made man, He made man different from the way He made all the other creatures of the earth.

> *And the LORD God formed man of the dust of the ground, and breathed into his nostrils the breath of life; and man became a living soul.*　　(Gen 2:7)

This passage says that God breathed into his nostrils the *"breath of life."* This phrase *"breath of life"* actually means "the *life of God.*" God didn't just make man, He breathed into man. The passage goes on to say that as a result of God breathing into man the breath of life (life of God), that man became *a living soul.* This phrase *"living soul"* is actually the phrase *"speaking spirit."*

When God breathed into man, He didn't just breathe empty air into Adam. God does not have the same anatomy as man, and He does not need to breathe air to exist. When He breathed into Adam the *"breath of life,"* this phrase *"breath of life"* actually means *"the life of God."* In other words, what God breathed into Adam was a little bit of Himself—His Spirit.

This is what separates man from animals. Animals are bi-part beings. They have a soul and a body. The soul consists of the mind, the emotions, and the will. Animals have a mind, and they have limited emotions and a limited, independent will. However, they do not have a spirit. God created them, but He never breathed into them—giving them a spirit. Man however is a tri-part being. Like animals, we have a body and a soul; but in addition, we also have a spirit. The spirit is what God breathed into Adam.

This is why we can never die. Our bodies will some-day die and decay, but the real you (which is your spirit) can never die because it is from God and of God. No part of God can ever die. People who commit suicide think they are ending it all. But they are not ending any-thing but their existence in the physical body. Their spirit and soul is going to live forever somewhere (heaven or hell).

Speaking Spirits—The Image of God

You must understand that God is a spirit. But He is not just any old spirit, He is a speaking spirit. When God created the earth and the universe, He didn't do it with His hands; He did it by speaking things into exis-tence with the power of His Word.

And God said, Let us make man in our image, after our likeness: and let them have dominion over the fish of the sea, and over the fowl of the air, and over the cattle, and over all the earth, and over every creeping thing that creepeth upon the earth.

Gen 1:26

This passage says that God created us in His image. This does not mean that God looks like humans. God had to create us with our human features in order to live and maintain on the earth. The image of God that this passage is referring to is God's tri-part image — spirit, soul and body.

The soul of God is the Father — the true image of God. The Spirit of God is the Holy Spirit. The Body of God is His Word. In the New Testament His Word takes upon flesh and becomes Jesus Christ.

Being made in the image of God means that we also have a body, soul and spirit. And, just as God is a speaking Spirit, because we are made in His image, we are also created as speaking spirits.

Even though we cannot create and form physical worlds with our words, because God created us as speaking spirits, we can form our worlds (our lives and circumstances) with our words. We literally form and shape our worlds (lives) by the words we speak.

Many people (not knowing the power of their words) have literally destroyed their lives, as well as the lives of others by the words they have spoken. On the other hand, many have also formed and shaped blessings and prosperity in their lives by the words they have spoken.

The Two Trees

There were many trees in the Garden of Eden, but there were two primary trees—the tree of Knowledge of Good and Evil and the Tree of Life. The tree of Knowledge of Good and Evil did exactly what its name stated. It brought not only knowledge of good unto Adam and his spirit, it also brought evil and the access of evil and sin to Adam and his spirit, and thereby to mankind.

Prior to Adam eating from the tree, his spirit was whole with God, sinless, and untouched by evil or sin. At that point Adam had daily and intimate commune with God because his spirit was pure and sinless like God. But after Adam ate of the tree, sin now had access and contact with his spirit.

Because of this new contact with evil and sin, Adam now had sin in his spirit. God had warned Adam that he would die if he disobeyed and ate from this tree. And just as God had warned, he died. First of all, Adam died spiritually. Spiritual death is a separation from God. God is pure and holy. He cannot come in contact with sin of any kind. And since Adam's spirit now had sin, God had to separate Himself from Adam (and mankind). This is the reason why Jesus had to come—to become a bridge between a sinless God and sinful man. In addition to spiritual death, it also began (the cycle of) many other hardships in Adam's life and in the life of mankind. It brought sickness, disease, pain, sufferings, physical death, and many other tragedies of life.

On the other hand, Adam could have eaten from the *Tree of Life*. The purpose of the Tree of Life in the garden was to be a source for Adam's strength, healing, provisions, and anything else he needed. Eating from this tree would have meant that he would not have to die, get sick, go hungry, or have any needs in life. This tree (The Tree of Life) was to serve God's purpose for providing everything Adam needed.

When Adam sinned by eating from the wrong tree, God had to get them out of the garden before they ate of the Tree of Life. Had Adam eaten from the Tree of Life after he had sinned, he (and all of mankind) would have been doomed to spend eternity in Adam's sinful state with no possible chance for salvation or redemption.

The Spiritual Trees

Even though Adam is long gone and we are no longer in the Garden of Eden, these two trees still actually exist. No, there has not been some secret excursion where someone has found the hidden Garden of Eden; it now exists in our mouths. Look at the following passage:

> *A wholesome tongue is a tree of life: but perverseness therein is a breach in the spirit.*   (Prov 15:4)

Again, there were many trees in the Garden, but two primary trees (The Tree of Knowledge of Good and Evil and the Tree of Life). Just as Adam chose from the wrong tree that brought him pain, trouble, sickness, disease and physical and spiritual death, he could have just as easily chosen from the right tree — the Tree of Life, which would have brought him healing, blessings, provisions and prosperity instead.

According to the above passage, our mouths are now the source of these two trees. Whenever we lie, backbit, gossip, murmur, complain or speak evil, negative, or ill-will towards or about someone, we are choosing to eat from the same tree Adam did — the tree of Knowledge of Good and Evil.

On the other hand, whenever we speak positive, blessings, and the Word of God, we are eating from the Tree of Life — the tree that is the source of our blessings. This is what the following passage illuminates:

> *I call heaven and earth to record this day against you, that I have set before you life and death, blessing and cursing: therefore choose life, that both thou and thy seed may live.* *(Deu 30:19)*

In this passage God says that He has set before us two different sources. These two sources are the two trees. One of them brings death and curses, and the other brings life and blessings. Because of the authority that God has given unto us as speaking spirits, every time we speak over our lives or over the lives of others, we are using the source of one of these two trees, and we will therefore get one of the two results. We will either get what Adam got (death and curses), or we will get what Adam could have received (life and blessings).

Can We Place a Curse On Someone?

By now we should clearly understand two things about man regarding our mouths: First, we should understand that we have the same two sources (trees) that Adam had to choose from. Secondly, we should understand that we were created as speaking spirits, and that through our words (choosing from the two trees), we can form and change our worlds and circumstances, and the worlds and lives of others by the words we speak.

Understanding this, we can now go back to answer the initial question we asked in the beginning of this chapter: Can we as Christians speak curses over people? First, let us establish exactly what is a curse. Simply put, a curse is anytime a person speaks or pronounces negative, ill-willed, or evil words or phrases over a person's life.

Most people think that only witches and sorcerers can put a curse on someone. But that's not exactly true. Because of the power of our words (as speaking spirits) Christians can (ignorantly) use that power in the negative to put a curse on someone's life just as effective as a witch or sorcerer.

The power and authority that God has given to man as speaking spirits work no matter how you use it. It's like someone giving you a knife; you can use it for good or bad. The knife can be either used for the good of cutting and preparing food, or it can be used for evil to either injure or kill someone. The knife doesn't cease to work because a person uses it for evil. It's up to the user how they choose to use it.

> *Death and life are in the power of the tongue: and they that love it shall eat the fruit thereof.*
> *Prov 18:21*

This passage tells us that we can either speak death into someone's life through our words, or we can speak life (blessings) into their lives. Even as Christians, we can still speak death, which is to curse someone's life through our words. It's like the example above of the knife. Just as the usage of the knife is entirely up to the user, whether we use our tongues for death or life is also entirely up to the user.

It was not God's intention for us to use the power and authority of our tongue to bring injury and destruction to each other, as well as ourselves. But Satan is the god of perversion. He takes things that were meant for good and blessings and changes the use and intentions of them to evil and destruction. This can be seen in any aspect of life.

Again, God said that He has set these two trees before us. But He goes on to tell us which one to choose from. Let us make a choice to choose from the right tree by speaking the right things, and thereby receive God's blessings.

Is Profanity Harmless?

Many in our society say that the use of profanity is harmless. They say that profanity is only harmful to the ears of those who are self-righteous, extremely objective and oversensitive, and those who want to censor the rights of others. Could this possibly be true?

As Christians, we must be careful not to allow the influence of the world to form our opinion of a matter. If we are going to develop opinions on moral and social issues of our time, we must go to God and to His Word to find out how He feels about these matters. So let us go to God's Word concerning this subject:

> *Ye have heard that it was said by them of old time, thou shalt not kill; and whosoever shall kill shall be in danger of the judgment: But I say unto you, that whosoever is angry with his brother without a cause shall be in danger of the judgment: and whosoever shall say to his brother, Raca, shall be in danger of the council: but whosoever shall say, thou fool, shall be in danger of hell fire.*
>
> *Mat 5:21-22*

Profanity In Jesus' Day

In Jesus' day (the days He walked on the earth), the word *"Raca"* (which means dumb, stupid, or empty-headed) was as strong a curse word as some of the four letter words we use today. Jesus said that the use of this word (as well as other curse words of that time) could cause a person to have to face the council. This council Jesus is referring to is the council of the Pharisees and Sadducees.

Even though the Pharisees became wicked, self-absorbed, unrighteous men, their original job was to help enforce the laws of God. The council could have had a person severely punished for saying words like this. Many were even flogged (whipped) for the use of this and other types of profane words of their day. And, this act of discipline was completely endorsed by God and the scriptures.

If that wasn't enough to convince a person of that day not to use profanity, Jesus went quite a bit further. He went on to say that whoever called his brother a *"fool"* would be in danger of hell. Let me just emphasize this point. Jesus is saying that the constant use of pro-fanity can cause a person to actually go to hell.

Jesus used the word *"fool"* as a light word. In our day, the word *fool* wouldn't even register on the profanity Richter scale. Just as it is a light word used in our day, it was somewhat the same in that day (compared to other words they used). The emphasis Jesus is making here is not the word itself, but the penalty that can come upon a person for using profanity. What He was saying is that if the use of what we would call a mild word like *"fool"* could cause a person to actually go to hell, how much more could the use of other, more severe profane words endanger a person spiritually.

So now I ask again the question I asked in the beginning of this topic: Is the use of profanity harmless? Only if you don't value what God feels and thinks about your use of it, as well as your eternal salvation.

Why Does God Hold Profanity So Serious?

Now that we know God's opinion on the use of profanity and the spiritual endangerment we can fall into when we use it, the question now becomes this: why does God hold the use of profanity so serious and destructive? It's because of the source. Let's look at the previous scripture we used earlier once again:

> *Ye have heard that it was said by them of old time, Thou shalt not kill; and whosoever shall kill shall be in danger of the judgment: But I say unto you, that whosoever is angry with his brother without a cause shall be in danger of the judgment: and whosoever shall say to his brother, Raca, shall be in danger of the council: but whosoever shall say, thou fool, shall be in danger of hell fire.*
>
> Mat 5:21-22

Before Jesus goes into the penalties and spiritual dangers of the use of profanity, He gives the reason why it is so dangerous—the source. The source is the spirit of anger. The spirit of anger is a very dangerous spirit to have upon you. Let's look at another passage:

> For *rebellion is as the sin of witchcraft*, and stubbornness is as iniquity and idolatry. Because thou hast rejected the word of the LORD, he hath also rejected thee from being king. (1 Sam 15:23)

In this passage God tells us that rebellion and stubbornness is as the sin of witchcraft. Anger and rebellion are spiritual cohorts. Whenever you find one, you usually find the other not far away. Anger and disgruntlement is what leads to rebellion.

This form of witchcraft does not come because someone placed a spell upon you; it comes from allowing and opening up your spirit to be used by another spirit. This passage goes on to say that this spirit causes a person to *"reject the Lord."* Whenever a person rejects the Lord and His Spirit, they automatically accept and receive another spirit.

There are (primarily) only two spirits operating in the world—the Spirit of God and the spirit of Satan. When people express themselves with the use of profanity, the source or root of their emotions and words are never, ever from the Spirit of God. You never see the fruit of the spirit of God in operation when a person uses profanity. It is usually motivated by anger, fury, rage and malice (spirits of witchcraft). As Christians, we can have God's Spirit within us, and yet operate in another spirit:

> *And when his [Jesus'] disciples James and John saw this [that the people rejected them], they said, Lord, wilt thou that we command fire to come down from heaven, and consume them, even as Elias did? But he turned, and rebuked them, and said, ye know not what manner of spirit ye are of.*
>
> *Luke 9:54-55*

In this passage the disciples became angered at the people because they rejected them. Because of their anger, they asked Jesus to allow them to call down fire from heaven to destroy them. But Jesus rebuked them and asked them if they were even aware that they were operating under the influence of another spirit. This spirit was actually the spirit of Anger.

Again, even though we can have God's spirit within us, we can still give ourselves over to another spirit that (momentarily) overcomes, consumes, and even controls us. Jesus rebuked the disciples because they didn't even recognize that this was happening to them, and that they were operating in another spirit (the spirit of witchcraft).

This spirit was the root motivation of why they wanted to destroy the people. It wasn't because of righteous indignation that they wanted to destroy (kill) them; it was because the people rejected them. It was their personal pride and arrogance of being offended that they wanted to kill them.

Like the disciples, when this spirit comes over us, we forget who we are and whom we represent (Christ), and we are taken over by a spirit of murder. The disciples wanted to kill and destroy them physically. When we use profanity, it's through the spirit of anger and the profane words we use that we are attempting to destroy (kill) them. It's the same spirit that caused Cain to kill his brother Able. Because of Cain's jealousy, he hated his own brother to such a degree that he killed him. When we use profanity (through the source of anger) we are doing the same thing with our words (attempting to destroy or kill the person).

That's exactly the same practice as witchcraft. Witches and sorcerers use witchcraft to manipulate, hinder and destroy their enemies and people who oppose them. When someone uses profanity, they are doing the same thing, with the same spirit.

WITCHCRAFT

*And to the angel of the church in Pergamos write;
These things saith he which hath the sharp sword
with two edges...I have a few things against thee,
because thou hast there them that hold the <u>doctrine
of Balaam</u>, who taught Balak to cast a stumblingblock before the children of Israel, to eat things
sacrificed unto idols, and to commit fornication.*

Rev 2:12-14

In the beginning of this chapter we began with the
above passage with Jesus rebuking the church of Pergamos for practicing the *Doctrine of Balaam*. This was not
simply a practice that Jesus disliked; it was something
that He hated and strongly rebuked this church for
practicing.

We gave the two aspects of the Doctrine of Balaam.
The first thing the Doctrine of Balaam represents is the
first thing that Balak attempted to get Balaam to do,
which was to curse God's people. We have established
that even though we are Christians, we can misuse our
God given authority to actually place a curse on our
lives and the lives of others.

In our next chapter we will begin the second aspect of the Doctrine of Balaam—Christians practicing witchcraft. After Balak could not entice Balaam (through money) to curse God's people, he resorted to a different scheme. He further enticed him with more money until Balaam gave in and taught Balak how to get God's people to actually bring destruction upon themselves through the practice of witchcraft.

In this chapter we will discover how that the use of profanity is actually the practice of witchcraft.

What Is Witchcraft?

The dictionary's short definition of the word *witchcraft* is the art and practice of a witch or sorcerer. To understand this, you must then come to understand what a witch or sorcerer is: they are people who use spells and incantations to manipulate people, influence their will, hinder, injure or harm them.

There are many ways a person can get involved in witchcraft. It can be done through seeking mediums such as with fortunetellers and séances. It can also be done through playing and experimenting with demonic games such as dungeons and dragons, playing with tarot cards, Ouija [*weedgie*] boards, and hundreds of others out there.

Some people know what they are getting involved in when they get involved in these games, activities and practices. However, many are totally ignorant as to their spiritual involvement. When they experiment in these activities, they are actually contacting and conjuring up evil spirits. And, through the contact of these demon spirits, they are actually bringing up an evil presence and influence upon their lives.

Although they do not realize that they are getting involved in witchcraft through these activities, they are. Any time a person contacts demon spirits (knowingly or unknowingly), through any source, or by any means, they are getting involved in witchcraft.

Witchcraft And Profanity

When a person uses profanity (even though they do not know what they are doing), they are doing the exact same thing—getting involved in witchcraft. Just as witches and sorcerers use words, spells and incantations to bring up evil spirits for their evil purposes, profanity does the same thing.

The words that are used in profanity are not merely empty, vain words with no meaning or impact; these profane words are calls for demon spirits. They are calls for specific evil and demonic spirits to come and bring a specific spirit or presence over the person that is targeted. They are also short, compact witchcraft curses and spells that impact, cause harm, and cause physical and spiritual hindrances and destruction in the lives of those at whom the words are aimed.

Most people would never in their wildest imagination consider themselves a witch or sorcerer evoking demon spirits to come and place an evil spirit or presence upon a person's life; but for the involvement in witchcraft and evil spirits that these words induce, they might as well put on a pointed hat and get on a broomstick.

There are many harmful things we do out of ignorance. And the practice of witchcraft through the use of profanity is definitely one of them.

> *My people are destroyed for lack of knowledge: because thou hast rejected knowledge, I will also reject thee...* (Hosea 4:6)

This passage shows us that it is because of a lack of knowledge that many of God's people are destroyed. It's because of a lack of knowledge in the spiritual realm that many of God's people are practicing the (secondary part of) the Doctrine of Balaam — Christians (ignorantly) using the practice of witchcraft to manipulate, hinder, harm, and even destroy each other.

In our next three chapter we are going to explore many of the words we commonly hear used as profanity in our society. We are also going to give the origin of many of the words, and how they have evolved into what they are today. As we explore the true (spiritual) meaning of these words, and the dark, occultist practice we are getting involved in when we use them, we will also find that they are not simply empty words, but rather, the use of a very (spiritually) dangerous, and detrimental, evil and satanic practice.

Through showing the meaning of each profane word, and the specific kind of demon a person is calling upon when they use them, it is my prayer that after learning the truth of what you have been saying and doing, that you will repent of your usage of these words, and through prayer, purge them from your vocabulary, as well as from your heart, mind and spirit.

* Exclaimer:

Please note that the following chapters will include some graphic language and profane word and their acronyms. The use of these words is necessary in order to give the reader the understanding of what is actually being used. If you are under the age of 18, or are easily offended by the use of profane language, and prefer not to be exposed to them, please do not read any further.

Chapter 2

SEXUAL PROFANITY

INTRODUCTION TO
SEXUAL PROFANE WORDS

In our English language, many of our words of profanity have some type of perverted sexual connotation associated with it. There is a reason for this. Let's look again at our foundational scripture:

> *And to the angel of the church in Pergamos write. I have a few things against thee, <u>because thou hast there them that hold the doctrine of Balaam</u>, who taught Balac to cast a stumblingblock before the children of Israel, to eat things sacrificed unto idols, and <u>to commit fornication</u>.* (Rev 2:12-13)

As we stated in chapter one, it was Balaam who taught Balak how to destroy God's people. Although he could not curse them, he taught Balak how to do it through seduction and fornication.

Again, it was the spirit of fornication and sexual immorality and disobedience that Balaam used to teach Balak how to destroy the Israelites. It's the same spirit of fornication that is the driving force behind the use of many of our sexually based profane words of today.

In this chapter we will look at some of these words, their origin, meaning, and the spiritual implications that are involved when we use them.

39

Spiritual Fornication

The Greek word for "fornication:" is "pornea", which means harlotry. The Bible defines this term as sexual immorality, or sex outside of God's covenant of marriage. Physical fornication is when a man enters a woman and becomes one with her in a sexual, sinful, non-covenant act.

In the same manner, spiritual fornication is when a person allows spirits (other than God's Spirit) to come upon them and even enter into them. This can happen through either demonic possession, or a person allowing different spirits to control and inhabit their lives. This can also happen through a host of other things such as getting involved in demonic activities and games, watching certain movies and videos, being in certain atmospheres, getting involved in sexual sins and perversions, or simply being negligent in the spiritual realm and not carefully guarding your spirit..

Spiritual Adultery

Spiritual adultery is the same as spiritual fornication with one exception. The difference is when the person is born-again and has God's Spirit within them. Again, fornication is sex between two unmarried people in a non-covenant, sinful, sexual act. When we become born-again, God places His Spirit within us and we become His bride. So spiritually, we become married to

Him. Since God is a Spirit, when He comes to inhabit and dwell within us, we become one with Him in the spirit. We are His. We belong to Him. And, as a committed bride, His spirit should be the only spirit we allow upon us or within our spirit. But when we allow other spirits to come upon us, or dwell or live within us, we are committing a type of spiritual adultery against God.

> *Know ye not that your bodies are the members of Christ? Shall I then take the members of Christ, and make them the members of an harlot? God forbid. What? know ye not that he which is joined to an harlot is one body? For two, saith he, shall be one flesh. But he that is joined unto the Lord is one spirit. Flee fornication. Every sin that a man doeth is without the body; but he that committeth fornication sinneth against his own body. What? know ye not that your body is the temple of the Holy Ghost which is in you, which ye have of God, and ye are not your own?* (1 Cor 6:15-19)

Both spiritual fornication and adultery carry with it a joining of spirits. When a person commits these sins there is a joining of their spirits together. When they join spirits, they become one. Therefore, whatever evil spirit or ungodly habitual habits or characteristics that may be on one person is some times transferred to the other person. These evil spirits sometimes do not manifest themselves for many years.

THE "F" WORDS

F_ _ _
&
F_ _ _ YOU

When someone uses these terms, it is a demonic summons for evil, demon spirits to have spiritual sexual intercourse with them or the person to whom they are aiming or speaking these words. It is a *general* call for all kinds of unclean spirits to move in and out of them at will. If that person's spirit is open and not carefully guarded, demon spirits will come up (upon the use or request of these words) and attempt to dwell upon and within them.

> *When the unclean spirit is gone out of a man, he walketh through dry places, seeking rest, and findeth none. Then he saith, I will return into my house from whence I came out; and when he is come, he findeth it empty, swept, and garnished. Then goeth he, and taketh with himself seven other spirits more wicked than himself, and they enter in and dwell there: and the last state of that man is worse than the first. Even so shall it be also unto this wicked generation.* (Mat 12:43-45)

This passage is describing someone who has an unclean spirit in them. The first characteristic about this spirit is that it comes and goes in and out of the person at will (spiritual fornication or adultery). The second characteristic about this spirit is that not only does it come and go at will, it also brings other, more wicked spirits with it.

Because these spirits are moving in and out of them, the person's spirit and character begins to change. As their spirit and character changes, they begin having mood swings and extreme behavioral changes. Eventually their lifestyle will also begin to change. But even more dangerous is the fact that these unclean spirits open the door for other, more wicked spirits to also come in and dwell within the person.

SPIRITUAL RAPE

When these spirits come in, it is not a smooth transition or entry. In addition to this word having sexual implications, it also carries a meaning of having forceful, violent sex. It's the same spirit that causes people to get involved in sexual bondage and sadomasochism (people who enjoy inflicting or receiving pain during the process of sex). It's also the same spirit that drives a man to rape a woman. When this spirit is called upon with this word, it comes forcibly and literally rapes their spirit and begins to forcibly take over.

That's bad by itself; but it's not the worst of it. Again, as the above passage also explains, when this spirit forcibly comes in, it also brings in other spirits that are more wicked than itself. It specifically draws sexually perverted spirits, but they also open the door to other evil spirits to also come in as well.

The most frequent use of this word is when someone uses it towards someone else as an expression of their anger towards them, or as a means to defame, insult or degrade them. It is also used by a person referring to themselves when they want to express personal frustration. Finally, it is used as slang for sexual intercourse. Regardless of how it is used, it has the same evil incantation and request for demon spirits to come upon their lives and the lives of the intended target. But, like most of these profane words used in this book, when these words are used, not only do they invoke these spirits upon the intended person to whom it is targeted and aimed, it also doubles back and comes upon the spirit of the person who is speaking these words.

MOTHER F_ _ _

In the previous topic we discovered that when the word F--- is used, it is a call for evil spirits to come upon that person, and to have forced spiritual intercourse with their spirit. We also discovered that it also opens the door for other, more wicked spirits to also come upon that person. Since this profane phrase (M.F.) is a derivative of the profane word, F---, it carries the same spiritual incantations when it is used, plus the following:

This word carries the meaning of incest. The description of this word is when a mother (or father) has sexual relations with their child. Even in an amoral, godless society, this act is despised by just about everyone. Most people, even atheists would cringe even at the thought of hearing someone do this unthinkable act. And even the most ardent opponent of prisons and cruel punishment would like to see this kind of person punished in the worst, most cruel and crude way possible.

A person who commits incest is a person who has an unnatural, inordinate sexual attraction towards their patents or children. A person would have to completely cross and disavow all boundaries of their conscience in order to have sex with their children or parents. Most people would describe this person as being emotionally and spiritually sick.

When this phrase is used, it is a call for unclean spirits like the other word used in this topic; but in addition, it's also a call for demon spirits to bring with them spirits that cause a person to have inordinate sexual affections and attractions.

These unnatural tendencies include homosexuality, lesbianism, incest, pedophilia and a host of other unnatural, inordinate sexual desires. In recent decades, the increased numbers of people who are coming out of the closet and announcing that they are gay are staggering. The gay and lesbian agenda would have you to believe that these numbers were always there but were just hidden because they were in the closet. But the truth is that these numbers have grown and multiplied because of perverted spirits.

In 2 Timothy 3:1-2, it talks about the condition of man that will change in the last days. One of the things that God says will be on the dramatic increase is people that are *"without natural affection."* This is the same as *"inordinate affection."* This increase in inordinate sexual behavior is first of all because these inordinate perverted spirits are stronger than they were only a few decades ago. The second reason is because people are opening themselves up more to these spirits through sexual experimentation and other means such as demonic games, movies, and perverted media influences. Once these evil sprits get in their sprits, it begins to change everything about them. The person is deceived into thinking that they were born gay. But the truth is that their spirit has been hijacked by a perverted spirit.

In addition to people opening themselves up to these perverted spirits through sexual experimentation, many are being overtaken by these perverted spirits through spells and incantations brought upon by the use of this profane phrase. The more this phrase is used, the stronger the spirit comes over the person. The use of these words does not automatically mean that the person will immediately begin displaying some type of inordinate sexual affection, but what does happen is that the spirits begin getting stronger and stronger in their lives.

Again, this phrase is a call for evil perverted spirits to come over a person. We used homosexuality and lesbianism as an example, but it can draw any spirit of perversion to come upon a person.

THE "B" WORD

Most of us already knew that this term refers to a female dog. But before I get into the spiritual implications that this above term carries, I want to first address the term "dog" by itself. A dog is an unclean animal that will eat or lick virtually anything. In fact, the Bible makes a reference to the dog in the following passage:

> For it had been better for them not to have known the way of righteousness, than, after they have known it, to turn from the holy commandment delivered unto them. But it is happened unto them according to the true proverb, _the dog is turned to his own vomit again;_ and the sow that was washed to her wallowing in the mire.   (2 Pet 2:21-22)

In this passage God makes a reference to the characteristic of a dog's disgusting way of eating its own vomit. At the end of this passage it even compares a dog's eating habits to that of a pig. A dog will vomit, and then lick up its own vomit. It's one of few creatures on the earth that will do it. This passage refers to those who had once turned to God and rejected Satan, but then backslid and returned to their old sinful ways again.

This passage is not calling anyone a dog; but like many other passages in the Bible, it uses the characteristics of an animal as a comparison to the spiritual realm. This passage is comparing the regurgitation nature of a dog in comparison to a backslider.

To call someone a dog is to conjure up spirits that brings the regurgitation nature of a dog upon that person spiritually. This particular spirit causes a person to reject (regurgitate) things of normalcy and things that are clean, wholesome, righteous or godly, and begin to turn to just the opposite.

This spirit would cause a person who was raised in a wholesome Christian home with good ethics, morals, and standards in life, to completely do a turnaround and begin to do just the opposite.

In our American society, many of our young men have taken on the slang of calling each other *"dog."* This term was originally used by young men as slang to boast of their exploits in the number of women they are able to have sex. While young men are bragging about their conquests to other men, they often respond by saying, *"man, you ain't nothing but a dog."* This is a phrase that should be offensive and should be rejected. But because young men take this term as complimentary, they willingly accept and receive it. But along with accepting and receiving this term, they also receive the spirit that goes along with it.

Don't allow your young men to openly use this term. Teach them the spiritual implications of what they are both releasing on others and accepting upon themselves. Teach them to reject this term, and ask others not to refer to them in this term.

B_ _ _ _ or son of a B_ _ _ _

As we said earlier, most of us already knew that this term refers to a female dog. But what most people do not know is that it also refers to a female dog in heat. I love to watch nature pictures of animals and insects. One thing that is constant in nature is that the female is usually very selective about what male she chooses to mate with her. They are selective to get the strongest, healthiest, biggest, and best male in which to mate. This is done in order to increase the chances of passing these selective genes down to their offspring so that they may have a better chance of survival. In the animal and insect world, only the strongest survive.

Unlike most other animals and insects in nature, the female dog is not selective of her mate at all. Once she comes in heat, she will lift her tail up to whatever male comes her way. The male dog can be large or small, strong or weak, or even sickly. It doesn't matter with a female dog in heat.

To call someone this term is to evoke evil spirits upon them with the characteristics of a dog as described above in our first part, but in addition to these spirits, it also evokes the spirit of whoredom upon them. The spirit of whoredom is a demon spirit that causes a person to have an unclean, uncontrollable sensation of lust and lasciviousness. This spirit draws women (as well as men) to begin to hunger for many different sexual partners. One sexual partner cannot satisfy them; they feel the need to have many different partners. And, like the female dog in heat, the more this spirit overcomes and overtakes them, the less and less discreet they become about with whom they are lying down.

In our society, it is not uncommon to hear of adult women (and men) who have had more than five to ten different sexual partners in one year. Many have had much more than that. Some even have several different sexual partners during the same time. This same spirit not only causes physical sexual addictions, it is also the cause of mental sexual addictions such as voyeurism and pornography. This spirit of whoredom is not only prevalent with adults in our society, it is now widely practiced among high school adolescents and even elementary school children.

Through movies and other influences, our society as a whole is beginning to accept this kind of lifestyle and behavior as normal. But regardless of what society is teaching, this kind of careless sexual activity is not normal at all. It is brought on by this spirit of whoredom.

When this spirit comes over a person, they become driven by an insatiable lust for sex. They also become

blinded and desensitized to all the dangers and compli-
cations behind having casual sex. When a person has
sexual relations, they make a connection with that person physically, emotionally and spiritually. There is a
danger in all three of these areas in practicing casual sex.

Physically, there are the dangers of catching deadly
sexually transmitted diseases. Emotionally, it is gut-
wrenching to go from one sexual partner to another.
Because of the connection that is made with the heart,
people become hurt and suffer all kinds of emotional
scarring of the heart and emotions through fornication.

The biggest danger however is the danger spiritually.
We stated in the topic of fornication that because the
two are joined as one, whatever evil spirits are on one
person comes upon another.

It is said that when a person has sex with someone,
it's like having sex with every person those people have
also had sexual relations. This can amount to hundreds.
And, just as AIDS and other diseases are spread
through sexual contact, spirits are also spread through
sexual contact.

The driving catalyst behind our society's unquench-
able thirst for widespread casual sex is an evil spirit. It
is the spirit of whoredom. There are many factors that
can contribute to a person having this spirit. One of the
factors is this practice of the Doctrine of Balaam. This is
to cast spells on people by the witchcraft use of the "B"
words and phrases and other sexually profane words
and phrases.

Chapter 3

FILTH WORDS

S_ _ _ _
or BULL S_ _ _ _

This word or phrase is slang for either human or animal defecation. This waste is worthless and good for nothing. Therefore, the origin of its meaning was to also refer to someone as worthless or good for nothing.

This slang is not normally used in reference to a person. It is usually used in reference to a situation that is incorrect, unacceptable or intolerable. However, even though it is not being used in direct relation with a person, both the person speaking the words and the person, people or circumstances the slang is directed towards become affected by this demonic incantation.

In the natural realm, body waste material is very unclean, filthy, disgusting, and foul. When this word or phrase is used, the person using it is calling for unclean, foul spirits of filth. This particular unclean spirit does not necessarily mean that they will begin having poor hygiene and unsanitary surroundings (although it sometimes can); what it does is cause the person to begin to tolerate and even enjoy lifestyles, environments and atmospheres that they themselves once thought was nasty, filthy, and repulsive.

The Prodigal Son

And he [the prodigal son] went and joined himself
to a citizen of that country; and he sent him into his
fields to feed swine. And he would fain have filled
his belly with the husks that the swine did eat: and
no man gave unto him.   *(Luke 15:15-16)*

The above passage is taken from the parable of the Prodigal Son. This parable is a good example of what happens to a person who has this unclean spirit. To understand the depravity and degradation of this young man's plight, you must first understand that Jews of that day hated and even despised pigs. First, they did not eat any part of the pig whatsoever. Second, they would not touch or even go near them.

As this young man's life began to spiral downhill, he stooped so low that he found himself taking a job working with the pigs in their nasty, filthy surroundings. He also had to feed them their pig-slop. And, if that wasn't bad enough for him, he eventually got so hungry that he found himself eating the same slop the hogs were eating.

This is exactly what happens to a person once this particular unclean spirit has overtaken them. They begin to frequent places they once viewed as despicable. They begin to befriend and keep company with people whose lifestyle they once thought were disgraceful and appalling. And, they eventually (because of the influence, oppression and possession of this spirit) find themselves doing the very things they once despised and never could have even imagined they would do.

Along with these changes, their sexual desires and preferences also begin to change for the worse. They begin experimenting in all kinds of extreme sexual practices and perversions; and, because of the spirit that is upon them, they even begin enjoying them.

All of us have seen people make drastic changes for the worse in the company they keep, places they frequent, sexual preferences, sexual practices, and in their basic lifestyles. Most of the time we have attributed these kinds of changes to the person simply going though a phase of life. But most of the time it is not simply a phase of life, it's a spirit that has affected them — causing them to go through these dramatic changes.

Like most evil spirits, once this spirit comes upon a person, they themselves do not even notice the change. And even if they notice the change, to them the change seems almost normal. To them it's everyone else that is abnormal. This is because (again, like most spirits) Satan blinds them to the truth.

Blinded By The god Of This World

In whom the god of this world hath blinded the minds of them which believe not, lest the light of the glorious gospel of Christ, who is the image of God, should shine unto them. (2 Cor 4:4)

This passage tells us that it's the god of this world (Satan), who blinds their minds (to the truth about their lives and circumstances). They do not see the changes they are making as bad, wrong or evil. They see them as normal. This is the reason why gays and lesbians see themselves as normal. This same spirit has blinded their minds to see themselves and their sexual preference and lifestyle as normal, when in fact it is abnormal.

Once this spirit takes over a person's life, they cannot see the truth as everyone else sees it. It's like they are sleepwalking. They are seeing one dimension of life as Satan shows them, while everyone else sees the true reality of life around them.

This is also the same spirit that is associated with drug addiction. When someone takes drugs, they are voluntarily opening their spirit to demonic involvement. It's not the drugs that get them addicted; it's the spirit that is associated with the drugs that gets them addicted. Once they become addicted, this spirit blinds them to the truth about their addiction and condition. They see their lives as normal and their addiction as controllable, when in fact their life is anything but normal, and their addiction is uncontrollable.

In the parable of the *Prodigal Son*, it says that the man *"came to himself."* This phrase "came to himself" actually means *"his eyes were opened to the truth."* In order for his eyes to be opened to the truth, the blinding spirit that was upon him had to be lifted. In the parable, it was the father's prayers for his son that caused the spirit to be lifted — allowing him to see (the truth about his life and condition).

If you know of someone whose life has taken a dramatic change for the worst, know that it's probably not a phase of life; it's more than likely a spirit is involved. Don't simply pray that they change, because they cannot change until they can see the truth about their life and environment. Pray (like the story of the Prodigal Son) that Satan's blinding spirit would be lifted from them — allowing them to see the truth and become set free.

By now you are probably wondering, "does all this happen because someone used a curse word, or had a curse word spoken over them?" While there are many other spiritual factors that can cause this kind of change in a person's life, know that they come from the same spirit. And, using this word or phrase is one of several ways of inviting this spirit into a person's life.

A - -

This word was originally used for donkey. In fact, it is still used in the King James Version of the Bible as the word for donkey. This word was originally used as a slang word to describe someone whom they felt was dumb, stupid, or ignorant.

JACK A - -

The origin of this name is not difficult to figure out. It began by someone calling a person named Jack an A--. They were attempting to describe them as being dumb and stupid. The name caught on and eventually became slang.

When someone uses this word or phrase, what they are doing is conjuring up specific demonic spirits that comes to attack a person's mind. This spirit can be attributed to mental diseases and disorders such as strokes, brain cancer, schizophrenia, and Alzheimer's disease. It can also be attributed (through generational curses) to children being born with mental retardation and other birth defects.

* Note: The curse phrase **Dumb S---** also carries the same meaning.

A _ _   H _ _ _

In modern day slang, these two words have been combined in an entirely different meaning. The modern day meaning for this word would be to describe a person's rectum. This area is considered the most unclean, undesirable, foulest, filthiest part of our bodies. To call someone this name now would be to refer to them in the same manner — filthy, unclean, stinky, and undesirable.

The use of this word is similar to the use of our previous word. When someone uses this phrase, they are also conjuring up unclean spirits of filth. These spirits are some of the same spirits that are brought on by the use of our previous word. It conjures up spirits that causes a person to change their behavior completely. These spirits change their desire to do things they once thought was despicable and detestable. With this spirit upon a person, they can now do immoral and shameful acts physically, socially and sexually that they never even imagined themselves doing before. And, because these spirits blind a person of hearing the voice of God, they can now do them without conviction and without their conscience bothering them.

The use of this word also has a level of sexual deviance to it. It refers to the sexual conduct of two males together. The use of this word can bring spirits upon a person that leads to homosexuality and lesbianism.

P_ _ _ OFF
or
P_ _ _ _ _ OFF

This phrase is another commonly used phrase. It is even used by many Christians, and even pastors who use it out of ignorance, not knowing the true meaning of what they are saying spiritually.

The origin of this phrase comes from the meaning of being urinated upon by a dog. Dogs have been known for ages to urinate on things around them. They have been known to catch a human's leg every now and then. This is something that would anger even the most avid dog lover.

This phrase therefore became known as a phrase that means to be angered, irritated or annoyed by something. The slang for the word *urine* is to *pee*. The word pee eventually evolved into the slang word *piss*. The word changed but the meaning stayed the same. To say that something *p _ _ _ _ _ you off* is to say that you are just as angry as you would be if a stray dog urinated (peed) on you.

It would be one thing for a stray dog to urinate on you because he was following his primal instinct of warding off predators or marking his territory, but for a human to do it, that would be an entirely different story. That's something that would anger a person to no end.

To say that a person p_ _ _ _ _ you off would be the equivalent of saying that you are as angry as you would be if a person urinated (p_ _ _ _ _) on you. This takes the degree of anger, irritation, or annoyance to a level that is off the chain.

For this to happen physically would be total filth. Remember, there are different spirits associated with different words. Any time a term is used that relates to obscene or perverted sexual behavior, defecation or urination, it is from the same spirit. They are all from unclean spirits. These are spirits that causes a person to tolerate, like, or even love things, surroundings, people, and sexual behavior that the average person thinks (and even they once thought themselves) to be despicable, filthy, and repulsive.

To say that someone p_ _ _ _ _ you off is a call or incantation for these unclean spirits to spiritually come and urinate on you, which is to come and rest their unclean spirits and spiritual influence upon you.

To tell a person to "p_ _ _ off" would be like telling a person to go and urinate on someone, or to allow someone to urinate on them. There are actually perverted sexual deviant people who enjoy having their partner urinate on them prior to having sex. This sexual deviance (and other perversions like it) comes from unclean spirits.

* Note: Because of the law of spiritual association, any term that closely relates to this term, such as *"peed me off"* carries the same spiritual implications and invocations.

Chapter 4

BLASPHEMOUS AND DAMNATION WORDS

DAMN, DAMN IT, OR I'LL BE DAMNED

He that believeth and is baptized shall be saved; but he that believeth not shall be damned.

Mark 16:16

The word *"damn"* is a derivative of the word, *"damnation."* It is a theological word meaning "eternal punishment of hell." This word was also used outside the (Christian realm) to refer to someone whose life (circumstances and events) took a drastic and dramatic turn for the worse for them.

When this happened, some believed that God had placed a curse on them and was judging them for some type of sin. An example of this can be found in the story of Job, where his friends thought that all the horrible things that happened to Job's life happened because he was being judged (punished) by God for sin in his life.

The other school of thought that some assumed when drastic hardship came upon a person's life was that someone (a witch or sorcerer) had placed an evil curse on them. Therefore, this word *"damned"* became synonymous with the word *"cursed."*

The Self-Induced Curse

*Death and life are in the power of the tongue: and
they that love it shall eat the fruit thereof.*

Prov 18:21

In chapter one, we discovered that God has created
us as speaking spirits with the authority to form and
change our worlds (lives) by the words we speak. The
above passage is one of the passages we used in that
chapter exemplifying the fact that we can either speak a
blessing or curse over our lives and circumstances.

When someone uses the word *"damn"* or *"damn it"*, it
is the same as saying, *"be cursed"* or *"I place a curse upon
it."* The *"it"* is whatever situation surrounds the person
at that time they are provoked to use this word or
phrase.

The other profane words we have used to this point
are all calls for evil and demonic spirits to come and put
its evil presence or spirit on a situation or person. In this
case, the person themselves are requesting for their circumstances to be cursed <u>without any help from Satan or
evil spirits</u>. <u>It is a self-induced curse</u>. Again, this is done
because, as the above passage states, *"death and life is in
the power of our words."* We have the power to cause
blessings and prosperity to come upon our lives with
the right words we speak, and we also have the power
to bring death (curses) upon our own lives with the
wrong words we speak. So with this word or phrase,

the person is using their speaking spirit authority to pronounce a curse over their own lives or present situation.

Cursing Your Entire Life

When someone uses the phrase, *"I'll be damned,"* it is saying the exact same thing as above, only it is also requesting a curse to be upon their entire life. The first phrase asks for a curse to be upon the particular situation surrounding that person. When someone uses this phrase, it is asking for their whole life to be cursed. To say this phrase is the equivalent of saying, *"I be cursed,"* or *"I place a curse on my life."* With these words a person is putting a widespread curse on their life.

Many people have mistakenly blamed Satan for things that Satan had little or nothing to do with. They have blamed Satan for causing storms, troubles and trials in their lives, when in fact, some of the time these things have come upon them because they have (out of ignorance) asked for the trouble themselves. One of the ways we can bring trouble into our own lives is with this self-induced curse.

Speaking this word or phrase can cause dramatic changes for the worse in a person's life. It can affect anything and everything in a person's life such as their finances, job, marriage and even their health. Yes, using this word can even affect a person's health. Just think about it; it's possible that some of the sicknesses and illnesses we have faced in life have come because we have (through our ignorance of using this phrase) asked for a curse to come upon our bodies, bringing sickness and disease. In addition to asking for sickness and disease, it is possible that some of our trials we have faced financially, on our job, in our marriages, and with our family and children were not brought on by Satan, but because we asked for it ourselves through pronouncing this curse upon our own lives.

The additional danger is that this phrase not only brings a curse upon your life, it sometimes brings a curse upon those with whom you are connected—such as your spouse and children. So to ask for your life to be cursed is not only bringing trouble to your life, it can also bring trouble to your children and grandchildren through this curse. For more information on this subject, please refer to our book entitled, *"Too Blessed to be Cursed."*

We have enough to deal with already with Satan and demon spirits trying to attack and destroy our lives. Let us not give him any help. Let us end these self-induced curses and begin speaking the right words.

CURSING GOD
(G.D.)

The original use of this phrase was very similar to the previous word, *damn*. When someone's life took a dramatic change for the worst, it was assumed that they had sinned and God was punishing them for their sins. They would therefore use the phrase, *"God has d----- them,"* meaning, that God had put these things upon their lives to judge them. The way it was used was not a profane word at that time. Over the centuries the words were shortened and finally used the way it is now heard.

The way it is used now however completely changes the phrase—thus changing its meaning. Instead of saying *God has d----- a person*, people simply say G.D. When they use this phrase, what they are actually doing is cursing God. The meaning now means *"God be d-----."*

BLASPHEMY

Even though all of these profane words are evil and spiritually detrimental, this phrase is far worse than any of them for several reasons. First, it's because it is outright blasphemy. To disrespect God in any way, fashion or form is blasphemy by itself. But to actually curse God is the absolute worst thing a person could possibly do or say.

BLASPHEMY AGAINST THE HOLY GHOST

There are two types of blasphemy that is referred to in the Bible. The first type of blasphemy is called *"blasphemy against the Holy Ghost."* This is when a person knowingly and willfully commits or contributes the works of God to the works of Satan. It is also when a person (in full knowledge and awareness of what they are doing) curse God or His presence. This is the equivalence of cursing God to His face. It's one thing to say something about someone behind their back, but it's another thing to curse them to their face. This is exactly what this type of Blasphemy does. This type of Blasphemy is called the *unpardonable sin*. There is no forgiveness or remittance with this sin. It is forever unforgivable and will doom a person to eternal punishment in hell.

Many Christians have asked and worried if they have mistakenly blasphemed the Holy Ghost. You cannot mistakenly commit this sin. Again, in order to commit this sin, a person has to be in full knowledge of what they are doing, and do it with malice against the Living God. A person would have to be totally reprobate and demonized in their spirit in order to commit this type of Blasphemy. And, there would be no conviction in their heart for using these words of blasphemy.

BLASPHEMY AGAINST HIS NAME
(GOD D_ _ _)

This type of blasphemy is not completely and totally unforgivable like the first type of blasphemy we mentioned. A person who commits this type of blasphemy can ask and receive God's forgiveness. However, this type of blasphemy does have penalties.

In addition to cursing God being blasphemy, the use of this phrase carries the heaviest penalty and repercussions. God is all-powerful, sovereign and omnipotent. He cannot be cursed in any way, fashion or form by any person, being, force, power, or spirit. Any attempt to curse God comes back on the person who attempts to curse Him. Therefore, when someone curses God using this phrase, what they are actually doing is (with their own words) bringing a curse upon their own lives. It's very similar to the previous topic. In this topic we said that when someone says, "*I be damned,*" what they are actually saying is "*I be cursed*" or "*I put a curse on myself.*"

When someone uses this phrase (G.D.), they are doing the exact same thing. Again, because God cannot be cursed, when they attempt to curse God with this phrase, they are actually putting a curse on themselves because the curse automatically comes back on them. But it gets worse. Any attempt to curse God does not simply come back to them one fold, it comes back to them a hundred-fold. It gets even worse. Not only does it come back on them one-hundred-fold, it also comes back upon their children, relatives, and generation.

Now that you have an understanding of what is being said with this phrase, you should agree that this is one phrase that you should get completely out of your vocabulary.

BLASPHEMY AGAINST HIS HOLINESS

When I was a little boy growing up, my favorite television show was Batman. Robin, Batman's trusty sidekick would often use the word *holy* with an assortment of fill-ins to describe their current state of crisis. He would use phrases such as, holy mechanical trap, holy explosions, holy ball and chain, and so on.

As a little boy, this had no real significance to me. But later on in life as an adult, after becoming a Christian, it began to bother me more and more to hear this word use so commonly. One day I was listening to a song called, "You are Holy," referring to God as the Holy One. The Holy Spirit then revealed to me the spiritual understanding of the dishonor and blasphemy of what I had been hearing for so many years of my life.

Hallowed is a derivative of the word *"holy."* It means to sanctify, consecrate, venerate, highly respect and highly esteem. In one of the most basics of Jesus' teachings, He taught what is called *"The Lord's Prayer."* Even though this prayer can be prayed verbatim, the truest meaning of this prayer was in teaching His disciples key principles of prayer. After addressing God as our

Father, the very first thing Jesus taught His disciples (us) was to reverence, honor and respect God *(Hallowed [holy] be thy Name)*.

In Isaiah 6:1-3, Isaiah saw a vision of heaven and the throne of God. In that vision he saw seraphim angels which stood above the throne of God. These giant, powerful and mighty angels declare an eternal song and declaration of praise unto God. They constantly cry, *"holy, holy, holy is the LORD of hosts: the whole earth is full of His glory."* Think about it; the word they use in the presence of God to continually praise and glorify Him is the word, *"holy."*

Again, holy is a sacred and consecrated word used to praise and glorify God. Holy, or holiness comes from God; it is of Him; it is about Him; it refers to Him, and it is a praise unto Him. He is the Holy One, the only Holy One. Holy is a word that also signifies God's divine nature, His purity, His righteousness, power, glory, and His awesome presence. When the Bible uses the word *holy* in reference to people, a place or a thing, it is referring to God's presence on the people, place or thing.

So to use the word *"holy"* in any manner that does not exalt, honor, lift up His name, bless Him, reverence Him, and respect Him is one of the biggest sins that we can commit. It is blasphemy in the truest term. It is just as much blasphemy to use the word "holy" in a common, disrespectful or dishonorable manner as it is to use the name of the Lord in these same ways.

Even though using the word holy in a common, disrespectful and dishonorable manner is wrong, blasphemous and sinful, it gets deeper than that. To use the word holy in combination with a profane or curse word is far more sinful. It's the same equivalent as cursing God. Because it carries the same meaning, it also carries the same spiritual and physical judgment and consequences to the person who uses it.

God cannot be cursed by any words, actions, or powers by any person, spirit or entity in the universe. Since God cannot be cursed, when someone attempts to curse God with their mouth with the continued use of these types of words and phrases, they unknowingly bring a curse upon their lives, family, and circumstances. In Numbers 14:18, the Bible says that God allows curses to come upon those who hate Him. The use of these words and phrases is an expression of hatred towards God whether the person speaking them means it from their heart or not. However, the same passage also expresses God's mercy and forgiveness for those who are willing to repent and change.

Don't let the devil convince you that words have no meaning. With our words we can honor God or dishonor Him; we can respect Him or disrespect Him, and we can reverence Him or blaspheme Him. There is a saying that says, when you know better you do better. Now that you know better, pray that God will help you to do better and begin a life honoring and reverencing God, His name, and His holiness, rather than blaspheming, dishonoring and disrespecting Him.

CLOSE ASSOCIATION

The Avoidance Game

To avoid condemnation for using this word or phrase (G.D.), some try to simply change the pronunciation to justify their use. Instead of pronouncing God's name in this phrase, they attempt to pronounce the word, "*got*" instead of "*God*" in the phrase. The person who uses this alternative selection of words feels that although they have used profanity, they do not think they have cursed God.

The problem with this philosophy is that although they substituted God's name, they still fall into the same sin and spiritual penalty for using this phrase because of a spiritual law called the *law of association*.

In the natural realm, if someone commits a crime and someone else aids or assists them, the person who assisted them can be charged with the exact same crime even if they didn't commit the actual crime. For example, let's say a group of people attempted to rob a bank. Let's say one of them served as the driver of the getaway car. Even though the driver didn't actually go into the bank and attempt to rob it, the driver could still be charged with the exact crime as the actual bank robbers because of their part (association) with the criminals who actually went in the bank and attempted the robbery. In fact, in some extreme cases, if someone was killed in the robbery, all parties involved in the attempted robbery could also be levied with a charge of murder or manslaughter.

The spiritual law of association works the same way. If you closely and affectionately affiliate yourself with someone who has a spirit, or even a curse upon their life, you put yourself in a situation to also become part of their curse or penalty. A Biblical example of this can be seen in the following passage:

Achan's Family Association

And Joshua, and all Israel with him, took Achan... and his sons, and his daughters, and his oxen, and his [donkies], and his sheep, and his tent, and all that he had: and they brought them unto the valley of Achor...and all Israel stoned him with stones, and burned them with fire, after they had stoned them with stones.   *(Josh 7:24)*

Because of Achan's deliberate disobedience to God, the Israelites suffered defeat in a battle they should have overwhelmingly won. After it was revealed to them by God that a man by the name of Achan was the cause, they took Achan and killed him. But not only did

Achan die, everything that was closely associated with him including his spouse, children, and family members also suffered demise.

Many of us would look at this passage and feel that it was unfair to kill Achan's family since they had nothing to do with Achan's crime. But you must understand that the Old Testament is a physical picture of spiritual principals and laws of God. Just as Achan's family died because of their close association, we can also become affected by our close association to people with generational curses and people who have certain spirits upon them.

In the same manner, when we use words that have a close association with a profane word or phrase, it carries the same sin and demonic incantation as if they said the actual word itself. So in the use of this phrase "*got d_ _ _ _,*" even though the person substituted God's name with the word "got," because of the law of association, it still carries the same sin and penalty as if they said the actual word.

* Note: The phrase *"gosh darn"* and other similar types of words still fall under this *law of close association.*

Alternative Words

It is my prayer that after you have come to understand what you are saying in the spiritual realm when you use profanity, that you would totally eliminate the need or use for profanity from your vocabulary. However, if you need to use an alternative word to express your emotions, then select something that has no perverted meaning, and has no similarity to the sound or spelling of the actual profane word.

An example of this would be if someone accidentally hit their finger with a hammer; instead of saying "damn it," I have heard many use the word "man." It may not sound as melodramatic, and it may not express the physical pain you felt to others the same way, but it will keep you from evoking evil spirits and cursing your life.

DANG —A Close Association

I have heard children use this word a lot lately. I have even heard them use this word around their parents. Since it is not the actual word, parents allow their children to get away with using it. But because of the spiritual law of association, using this word carries the same demonic invocation as using the actual profane word in which it is associated.

So if you are a parent that has allowed your children to use this word, stop them immediately. Teach them that this is wrong and how it is actually associated to other words, and the fact that these words have demonic meaning.

Using God's Name In Vain

Not only is this phrase (G.D.) wrong because it is actually an attempt to curse God (blasphemy), it is also a direct violation of the fourth commandment. Breaking this commandment is no less serious with God than stealing or committing adultery.

Taking the name of the Lord in vain is not a demonic call for demons like the other words we have used thus far in this teaching. We've discovered that the other names are actually demonic spells and incantations used to call evil and demonic spirits to put a spell, spirit or curse upon a person.

Using God's name in vain does not do either one of those. However, to the person who uses God's name in vain, it can be just as harmful and destructive to them and their lives.

What is God's Name

In Genesis 15:1, Moses asked God what name he should give to Pharaoh for God. God responded by telling Moses to tell Pharaoh that *"I AM"* has sent you. God used this referenced name because He is (I AM) whatever we need. Whatever you need from God, just put it in the blank after "I AM" and that's what God becomes to you.

In Exodus 6:3, God later reveals Himself to Moses by the name of "Jehovah," which simply means *God*. The other Jehovah names were simply names that identified who God was to them in a particular situation. In other words, if you needed God to be a healer, you would call upon Him as *Jehovah Raphe*, which simply means *God, my healer*. There were many other Old Testament references that God gave His people to address Him such as The Almighty, The Sovereign God, the God of Abraham, Isaac and Jacob and many other name.

In the New Testament however, God brings us into His intimacy by telling us to call Him Father. Knowing God as the Almighty God or Jehovah makes it sounds like God is out there a million miles away. But "Father," let's us know He is with us, he loves us, He forgives us, and desires for us to be in His intimate presence.

However, when you use His name we must go through the name of Jesus Christ. In fact, no prayer to God is valid, accepted or even acknowledged by God that does not come through the name of Jesus Christ. The following are many of the names and references of God's names that He has given to us to refer to Him:

God, I Am, Jehovah, Jesus, Jesus Christ, The Lord, The Almighty, my Lord, and The Lord.

These are not all the names and references of God. There are many more. Basically, any name that God has given to us to use as a reference to Him or to call upon Him is sacred and should not be used in vain.

Common Usages of God's Name In Vain
"Oh my God" or "OMG"

In today's society people often use God's name in vain as if has no meaning, no purpose and just words. People also use God's name in vain as a common cliché or emotional expression when they are sighing, frustrated, tired, upset, angry, or shocked about something. People also commonly use God's name in vain in the heat of sexual passion. Using His name in vain in any of these instances is to reduce the name of the God down to a mere, common, casual expression — Blasphemy.

Examples of Using God's Name In Vain:

Saying, "God", "Oh God, " or "oh my God" or "OMG"

Saying, "Jesus" or "Jesus Christ!"

Saying, "Lord" or "my Lord" or "Lord have mercy."

It is not wrong to use these names and references of God. It's how you use them that makes it wrong. It is all right to use His name to *"properly"* address, reference, petition or worship Him, or in any way as long as it is in a manner that is respectful, honorable and reverential to Him. To use His name (s) for any purpose other than these is using His name in vain.

Disrespect to God

It is considered highly disrespectful for us to use the name of a ruler, president or monarch in a way that is unbecoming, common or obscene. We even give respect to our supervisors on our jobs, as well as local and national dignitaries by properly addressing them by their title when we speak to them or refer to them. As children (and even now as adults), we would not have even considered using our parents name in a way that was disrespectful to them.

God is the supreme ruler of the universe and all existence. He is holy, sovereign, almighty, all-knowing, all-powerful and omnipotent. He is the source of all things, the giver of all things and the sustainer of all things. If it is disrespectful for us to use the name of any mere earthly person of power, prestige or authority improperly, how much more egregious and a gross, sinful abomination it is to use the name of the Lord our God in a vain way, manner, or form.

> *Thou shalt not take the name of the LORD thy God in vain; for the LORD will not hold him guiltless that taketh his name in vain.*　　(Exo 20:7)

In the above passage, God says that He will not hold

the person *guiltless* who takes His name in vain. This word *"guiltless"* is actually the word *"unpunished."* God is saying this: Those who use His name in vain will not go unpunished by Him. I believe that this refers to a continual use of His name in vain without repentance. The continued use of His name in vain will cause God to judge us.

The scripture tells us that we reap what we sow. Sowing blasphemy will cause us to reap God's judgment in our lives just as much as sowing lies or adultery.

There are some things that come upon our lives as a result of Satan's attacks against us; however, there are some detrimental actions that come upon our lives as a result of our defiance, disobedience, and disrespect to God. Using God's name in vain can cause God to judge you in any area of your life. It may be financial, health, or any area. Many have attributed the devil to attacking their lives, when in fact it was God judging them for their continued disobedience. And using His name in vain is one of those things for which God will judge us.

Loosing Power and The Anointing

There are times when we do not have time to be formal in prayer. These are times of emergencies such as onset illness or injuries, sudden danger, and sudden fear or fright.

*For whosoever shall call upon the name of the Lord
shall be saved.*   *(Rom 10:13)*

This passage has a two-fold meaning. First, it refers
to salvation. Secondly, it refers to those who are in imminent danger.

*God is our refuge and strength, a very present help
in trouble.*   *(Psa 46:1)*

This passage expresses the same thing that the previous passage expresses. It expresses the fact that when
you are in imminent danger that you can call upon God
for help through calling upon His name. When you call
upon His name in times of trouble or distress, the angels of God come to your aid and assistance.

I have personally had many occurrences where I
have had to call upon His name when I was in immedi-
ate danger of being involved in an automobile accident
and other impending dangers. In each of these times
God's angels came to my rescue and delivered me from
the dangers. To this day I cannot explain how I avoided
some of these accidents and other dangers. Well, actually I can (in the spiritual realm), but not in the natural
realm. It was the angels of God that delivered me. My
testimony probably sounds familiar to many who are
reading this book. You may also have had similar ex-
periences of how God rescued you by calling upon His
name.

The Boy Who Cried Wolf

Not only is using God's name a sin and an abomination, it can also be very dangerous for you. Most of us have heard of the story of the *"boy who cried wolf."* For the few who haven't, let me give you a brief synopsis of the story. There was a young shepherd-boy in a village who (for a joke) went out among the villagers and shouted that a wolf was attacking his sheep. The men of the village ran to his rescue, only to find the boy laughing because he had done it as a joke. The same thing happened several times. Each time, like before, the villagers would come to his rescue and the boy would laugh at their vulnerability to his prank. Finally, an actual wolf attacked the sheep and the boy went and shouted that a wolf was attacking; but this time no one believed him and the wolf got away with the sheep.

To some degree, this is what happens in the spiritual realm. The angels of God are assigned to show up and deliver you when you call upon His name. Each time you call Him, they instantly come to your rescue. If you continually use His name in vain, there will come a time when (like the boy who cried wolf) you'll call upon the name of the Lord expecting the angels of God to come to your rescue, and they will not respond.

Imagine, driving in your car and out of your peripheral vision you see a car about to hit you from the side, and you call upon the name of the Lord. But this time the angels fail to come to your rescue because you have called the name of the Lord in vain so many times. That's exactly what can happen if you continue to use His name in vain. So for the sake of your life and family's lives, you need to stop this gross and dangerous sin.

Diluting The Anointing

Calling upon the name of the Lord does more than bring the angels of God to your aid and assistance; it also brings the anointing of God to your situation. In Psalms 68:1, it says that when (the presence of) God arises, His enemies (demons and devils) become scattered. It's the anointing of God to which this passage is referring. The anointing (presence) of God breaks and destroys the yokes of the devil.

The anointing of God is potent, powerful and mighty. But when you call upon the name of the Lord without purpose (in vain), what you are doing is diluting the anointing. Just as diluting medicine or any other type of chemical will lessen its potency and effect, the continued use of calling on God's name in vain will also lessen the effect of the anointing. This is what Satan wants. Diluting the anointing causes our prayers to become ineffective against demons and devils.

Our binding and loosening of Satan and demon spirits only work because of the anointing of God that is upon our lives and prayers when we use His name. But as we continue to disrespect His name and use it in vain, it dilutes the anointing. There will come a time when you will need the full potency and power of God's name to deal with devils and demons. But if you have diluted the anointing by using God's name in vain, you will be left without proper power and potency in your prayer, and you may suffer defeat because of it.

Don't be deceived. Satan would have us to believe that there is nothing wrong with us using God's name in vain. He wants us to believe that they are mere, harmless words that are only used as expressions. Don't let Satan deceive you. First, know this is a blatant sin. It's just as big of a sin and violation of God's Word as adultery, stealing, or any other commandment of God. And, to continue to commit this sin is punishable by God. Second, know that Satan uses this as a weapon against us and our prayer lives—causing our prayers to become ineffective against him.

If you have been using God's name in vain, stop it immediately. You can begin practicing using some other (innocent, non-related) words to express your emotions. If you do mistakenly use God's name in vain, repent immediately. Don't wait, don't delay, do it on the spot.

Complying with the directives of this topic will cause you to come from under the judgment of God for blaspheming His name, cause the angels to stay ready and alert when you need to call upon the Lord for help, and bring power and effectiveness (the anointing) back to your prayer.

HELL

And fear not them which kill the body, but are not able to kill the soul: but rather fear him which is able to destroy both soul and body in hell.

(Mat 10:28)

And in hell he lift up his eyes, being in torment...

Luke 16:23

Television often makes it seem as though Satan rules and reigns in hell. The devil is not in hell. He is a spirit that moves up and down in the earth causing deception and destruction. But the day will come when Satan will be cast into hell.

In Revelations 20:10 it describes a time in which Satan will be cast into the lake of fire (hell) forever. Isaiah 14:16 describes this time as a day when Satan himself will be stripped by God of all of his power, and reduced to a regular, helpless soul, who will spend eternity in hell's sufferings.

There is nothing glamorous about hell. It is a place prepared by God for Satan, his followers, and those who refuse to accept God, His Word, and His ways. It will be a place of eternal, bitter torment.

This is probably the most widely used of all the profane words. I even hear this word used by Christians who think nothing of using it (in a slang, non-biblical way). It's sad, but I have even heard well-known, respected pastors and televangelist use this word (as well as a few others) in the pulpit while preaching the Word of God. After they use these words, they usually attempt to justify their use of these words by saying something like, *"I'm just keeping it real."*

I have two major problems with this. First, how can a parent justify to their children that it is wrong to use profanity (of any kind), while the pastor—whom the children are taught to respect, use them. Secondly, it is a call for evil spirits, and should not be used out of biblical context at all, but especially not in the house of God.

How It Is Used

Like most profane words, people use it as an expression of their anger and frustration towards someone or something. People also use this word as an expression for extremes. The following are a few examples of how this word is often used:

Go to h---
I'm mad as h---
I'm tired as h---
Scared the h--- out of...

HELL—A PLACE OF TORMENT

As we have discovered, hell is a place of torment. When people use this word as a cliché, an emotional expression of extremes, or any other manner other than that in which the Bible intended, like the other profane words, it becomes a call for evil spirits. Again, hell is a place of torment; therefore, the spirits that this word calls upon are spirits that come to bring torment.

These spirits of torment does several things. First, they bring confusion. Confusion and torment comes from the same spirit. In 1 Cor. 14:33, it says that *God is not the author of confusion*. Since God is not the author of it, then it's only one other source—Satan. When these words are used, it becomes a summons for evil spirits to come and bring confusion, arguing, fussing and fighting to the situation at hand. To refer to someone as being "_____ as hell," brings these spirits upon them. These spirits cause people to have sudden mood swings of anger and rage. They quickly go from one end of the spectrum to the other for no apparent reason. They become hard to get along with, and will argue over just about anything in which someone disagrees with them.

The other attribute of this spirit is one of torment. This spirit robs them of their peace. Look at the following passage as a reference:

But the spirit of the LORD departed from Saul, and an evil spirit from the LORD troubled him. And

Saul's servants said unto him, Behold now, an evil
spirit from God troubleth thee.   (1 Sam 16:14-15)

The above passage is taken from the story of Saul
and David. Because of Saul's disobedience and rebellion
against the Lord, God took His spirit away from Saul.
When it says that it was an evil spirit from the Lord, this
spirit did not actually come from God. When God takes
His spirit away from a person, an evil spirit automatically comes in. This is what happened to Saul. Because
of this spirit, Saul was continually troubled in his spirit.
He did not have any peace, he could not rest, and he
continually had trouble sleeping. Saul experienced these
things because of this evil spirit. When someone uses
this word (hell) out of Biblical context, it is a call for this
same spirit to come upon them (and their situation) as it
did upon Saul.

We live in a time where people (including children)
need medication for everything. We need medication to
sleep, wake us up, calm us down, and even rest. There
are many circumstances in a person's life that can cause
confusion, sleeplessness, and restlessness, but many
times there is a spirit of confusion and torment involved.
Using this word is one of the ways that a person can get
this spirit into their lives.

God has not called us to confusion; nor has He called
us to be tormented by these spirits and robbed of our
peace. Put an end to these spirits and stop using this
word.

Chapter 5

THE ATMOSPHERE OF PROFANITY

THE ATMOSPHERE OF PROFANITY

Listening To Profanity

After reading this book thus far, you may be one of those who are breathing a sigh of relief because you are not guilty of using profanity. Thank God for His wisdom in you choosing not to use it. However, you are not quite out of the water yet. There is still a spiritual danger.

Still A Danger

Even though you may not be using profanity, it can still be a danger to you spiritually. The danger is in watching movies that are filled with profanity. As we will discover more in the following chapter, when you are properly covered by the Word of God and the Spirit of God, you don't have to worry about the witchcraft of profanity affecting you. This is indeed true unless you open up your spirit to it.

You see, (spiritually) there is a difference between a person being an unwillingly participant in something, versus a willing participant. The Bible tells us in John

17:14 that *"we are in the world but not of the world."* While we are in the world, we are going to be bombarded by the temptations, attacks, and influences of Satan. You can be around negative influences and close your spirit off to them. But when you willingly place yourself around them, it's a different story. Let's look at the following passage:

> *I will set no wicked thing before mine eyes: I hate*
> *the work of them that turn aside; it shall not cleave*
> *to me.* (Ps 101:3)

In this passage, it says *"I will set no wicked thing before my eyes."* What this passage is actually saying is that *"I will not [willingly] put any wicked thing before my eyes."* Again, when you are forced to be around a temptation or influence, you can still keep your heart and spirit guarded from the attacks and infiltration of your spirit by evil spirits. However, when you willfully watch a movie or place yourself in an adverse atmosphere, you inadvertently open up your spirit to its influences.

This is why movie producers can easily sway your feelings, emotions, and opinions about the content of a movie. They can make you feel sorry for the bad guys and despise the good guys. They can make you root for someone who is having an adulterous affair and despise the one with the wholesome married relationship. This is done through an assortment of movie techniques and gimmicks such as music, settings, lighting, and good acting. However, along with swaying your feelings and emotions, they can also influence your spirit. Again, this is done because when you willingly sit down to watch a movie, you also open your spirit up to its influence both emotionally and spiritually.

When a movie is produced, different types of spirits become drawn to that movie. These spirits are released over the airways to whoever watches the movie and open up their spirit to it. Movies that are filled with violence release the spirit of anger. Movies that are filled with women and men dressed provocatively and sensually, and having casual unmarried sex release spirits of lust. Movies that are filled with witchcraft release all kinds of demon spirits. These are just a few of them. There are a host of different kinds of spirits that are released with different kinds of movies. Along with these kinds of spirits, there are also spirits released through the constant use of profanity in the movie.

Again, as we will discuss more in the following chapter, if you are protected by the spirit of God and the Word of God, you don't have to worry about any evil spirits that are released upon you. But again, when you willingly watch a movie, you open yourself up to the spirits that are released through that movie. Therefore, even though you are protected by the Word of God and the Spirit of God, when you watch a movie, you are actually letting down the hedge and allowing those spirits to come upon your life.

I know that we live in a time where it is nearly impossible to watch a decent movie without hearing at least some kind of profanity. In fact, in Hollywood, if a movie is projected to be a rated G or PG movie, and it was not intended to be a children's movie, the producers will often add explicit profanity to the movie to boost the ratings up to rated R. They do this in order to sell more tickets, because many adult moviegoers will steer away from rated G movies — citing it as a kid's movie. Because of this, as well as a thirst by our society for movies that contain more and more graphic sex, violence, and profanity, it is very hard to find a decent movie out there. Because of this rarity, you will probably find yourself watching movies with some degree of profanity in it.

My first suggestion is that you allow the Holy Spirit to lead and guide you as you watch these movies.

Grieve Not The Holy Spirit

And grieve not the holy Spirit of God, whereby ye are sealed unto the day of redemption.   (Eph 4:30)

Because the Holy Spirit is in you, when you open up your spirit to watch movies, the Holy Spirit becomes grieved when (the constant use of) profanity and other offensive material to the Holy Spirit is released upon you through the movie. If the movie is bombarded with profanity to the point that your spirit becomes immensely grieved through this constant use of profanity, you may need to make a choice to leave the movie. This is something I've done many times.

There have been times that I have taken my wife to the movies, and the movie selection we made was so filled with vile profanity that I left from the movie. Whenever I've done this, I found the manager and asked if we could switch to another movie. They have always obliged me with no problem whatsoever. If you choose to leave a movie under these circumstances and would like to watch a different one, I don't think that you will have a problem either.

What Do You Do After You
Have Watched A Movie With Profanity?

Sometimes you can find yourself watching a movie and trying to struggle your way through a few offensive words and scenes in the movie, and before you know it, you have watched the entire movie. By this time your spirit is totally grieved, and your spirit is very heavy from the content of what you have both seen and heard.

Spiritual Heaviness

Some time ago I was doing some research on drugs. I wanted to make a spiritual correlation between the addiction of drugs and other spiritual addictions. Even though I've had many bad habits in my life, I have never taken any serious drugs before. I wanted to know specifically about crack cocaine, how people use it, and the affects it has upon a person's life. I asked my brother-in-law about it because he had been delivered from an addiction to crack cocaine about a decade ago. He explained some things to me, but suggested that I watch a particular HBO production DVD he had about the street life of crack and cocaine usage.

I asked him to let me borrow it to view. Before he gave me the DVD, he warned me that the language in the video was very offensive (which turned out to be an understatement). I watched the DVD and through it learned the information I was seeking. But in the process, I was exposed to some of the most vile, perverted language I had heard in a long time.

Immediately after watching the DVD, I felt extremely heavy in my spirit. I knew that this was the weighing of the spirits that was released from this video, as well as the spirits that was released from the profane language of this video.

Flush Your System

Before I moved from my seat, I began doing something I call "*Flushing Your System.*" Just as a commode becomes full of waste and needs flushing after a person uses it, your spirit can also become full of dangerous spiritual waste after viewing some movies and videos. Flushing your system is a term that I use for taking the Word of God and praying spirits of heaviness off of your spirit and your life.

Since my spirit was heavy after viewing this video, I began flushing my system. Through the authority of God's Word, I released the demonic spirits from my life and my household that came from the DVD. I commanded them to loose every grip, influence and attack. I rendered them all to be helpless, powerless, and ineffective to cleave to, or rest upon my life, home, and anything around me. This went on for quite a few minutes.

After praying that prayer, I felt a spirit of peace come upon me. I knew then that the evil spirits associated with that video had been lifted and dispersed. I said all of that to say this: If you find yourself watching a particular movie, and afterwards feel heavy in your spirit, it's because evil spirits have been released through the movie upon your spirit, and because of this, your spirit has become heavy and grieved. If this happens to you, you need to do the same thing I did — flush your system.

> *I will set no wicked thing before mine eyes: I hate the work of them that turn aside; it shall not cleave to me.* *(Ps 101:3)*

In the above passage I want to bring out the last part where David said, *"It shall not cleave to me."* When you watch movies that have spirits associated with it, it is necessary to flush your system with prayer. If you do not flush your system, the spirits that are released through that movie will *"cleave"* to your spirit. If they stay there long enough, they will begin to infiltrate your spirit and begin to affect your spirit-man and your life.

It is like going outside digging and doing yard work with your bare hands. It is necessary for you to thoroughly wash your hands after you finish. If you don't, you take the risk of later ingesting all kinds of infectious germs and bacteria. It's the same with the movies. If you do not flush your system immediately after viewing it, you take the chance of them getting into your spirit. Once they get into your spirit, they can then affect your life.

On Page 123 is another prayer. The first prayer on page 120 is a repentance prayer for someone who has been using profanity. The second prayer is for someone who has been in the atmosphere of others using profanity. If you find yourself getting spiritually dirty (being in an atmosphere where constant vulgar profanity is being used), don't allow these spirits to cling to you; flush your spirit with prayer and the Word of God.

Not A Free For All

This section on *"Flushing your spirit"* is not a license and *free for all* to just let yourself go and watch anything that comes on television, videos or in movies. Again, you have to use the caution of the Holy Spirit.

There are some movies and videos that can be extremely dangerous and detrimental to your spirit-man. First, you need to use some spiritual common sense. As a Christian, there are some movies that just shouldn't be watched at all. Movies that contain extreme or explicit sex or sex scenes, horror movies, and movies that deal with witchcraft of any kind should be totally avoided. Most of these types of movies can be easily detected by the title or previews.

There are other types of movies that can also be very dangerous to your spirit-man. They are movies that are immensely saturated with profanity, blasphemy, and nude scenes. They may not be as obvious from the title or preview, but after about five minutes into the movie, you should be able to easily tell what the rest of the movie is about. Then there are movies that are not so obvious from the title, previews, or the first five minutes, but yet become extremely grievous to your spirit. They are the kind of movies in which you are going to have to use the guidance of the Holy Spirit.

If you continually and frequently watch movies that grieve your spirit, it will become harder and harder to flush your system of the spirits from it. So use some spiritual discernment and discretion in your movie selection.

* **Note 1**: This section on "Flushing Your System" can also be used in the case where you are forced to be in an atmosphere where there is a lot of profanity used. This commonly happens on jobs, the military, and other places. In these cases, you can use the prayer on page 123 to also flush your system. In this prayer, when you

see the word "movie," simply replace it with the word "atmosphere."

- **Note 2:** For those who are interested, there are devices out there such as *ClearPlay* that will edit out profanity, nudity, and other offensive materials from your DVD movies. For more information, go to http://www.clearplay.com.

Chapter 6

WHAT DO
I DO NOW?

What Do I Do Now?

After reading this book, you are probably in a state of shock and total amazement as to what has been going on in the spiritual realm with the use of profanity. There are probably several questions running through your mind at this time. You are probably wondering, *"What do I do now?"* You are also probably wondering if it is even possible to stop using profanity. During this final chapter we will answer these questions.

If you truly receive the revelation that God has revealed to you through this book, and you want to turn, change, and stop using profanity, there are seven things you must do. They are as follows:

1. Repent
2. Cleanse Your Heart
3. Do not Walk in Fear
4. Begin Covering Yourself
5. Stop Using Profanity
6. Repent Again (if needed)
7. Reject Satan's Deception

1. Repent

If we confess our sins, he is faithful and just to forgive us our sins, and to cleanse us from all unrighteousness.

1 John 1:9

The first thing we should do when the truth is revealed to us about our sins is to repent. Many people make the mistake in attempting to justify their disobedient actions and sinful ways. The thing we should do when God shows us our sins is to repent. Repentance becomes an acknowledgement of the truth. The Bible teaches us that it's only when we acknowledge the truth (about God's Word and about ourselves) that we can become set free.

God wants to set you free from your involvement in witchcraft and demon spirits through your use of profanity. Once you are set free, your life will be free to receive the blessings that God has ordained for you.

At the end of this chapter you will find a repentance prayer for using profanity. Immediately after finishing this book, pray this prayer from your heart to the Lord. Through this prayer you will find God's mercy, grace and forgiveness. If after you finish reading this book, you later feel the need to come back and say this prayer again, feel free to do so. Repentance is your first key to deliverance.

2. Cleanse Your Heart

That he might sanctify and cleanse it with the washing of water by the word. (Eph 5:26)

As you pray this repentance prayer, allow the Word of God through this prayer to also cleanse and sanctify your heart and mind from the language that has been used in this book. Although we used abbreviations for many of them, because you knew what the words were, they may be still going through your mind. Even after you finish praying the prayer, quote a couple of scripture passages. A good scripture passage may be Psalms 91.

The above passage tells us that the Word of God sanctifies, cleanses, and washes our soul. Whenever you have been in an atmosphere that made your spirit feel uncomfortable (such as watching a movie, being involved in an argument, either using profanity yourself or being around the use of profanity, or anything else that made your spirit feel uncomfortable) wash and cleanse yourself with prayer and the Word of God.

3. Do Not Walk In Fear

I know of Christians who walk under a continual cloud of fear. They are fearful that there is a witch or sorcerer who works with them that has put a spell on them. They are afraid to eat anyone's cooking or even eat at a restaurant because they are afraid that someone may put something in their food—thereby putting a spell on them. Some are even afraid to go out in public because of a fear of curses. For some, this paranoia just goes on and on. This is not the kind of life for which God has called us. He has called us to a life of peace. Even though there are many out there who do practice witchcraft, voodoo, and black magic, we do not have to walk in fear of them.

> *For God hath not given us the spirit of fear; but of power, and of love, and of a sound mind.*
>
> *2 Tim 1:7*

In the above passage God says that He has not given us a spirit of fear. A spirit of fear is exactly the kind of fear that is demonstrated in the passages above. It's the kind of person who is fearful and paranoid of a demon spirit being in everything.

> *The wicked flee when no man pursueth: but the righteous are bold as a lion.* (Prov 28:1)

The spirit of fear is exactly what this passage describes. It is to be afraid when there is nothing to be afraid of. When you are covered by the Spirit and Word of God, you don't have to be afraid. Don't walk in the spirit of fear. As this passage tells us, walk *"as bold as a lion,"* knowing that because of the protection of God (that is upon your life), nothing can touch you.

112

> *No weapon that is formed against thee shall prosper;*
> and *every tongue* that shall rise against thee in
> judgment thou shalt condemn. *This is the heritage
> of the servants of the LORD, and their righteous-
> ness is of me, saith the LORD.* (Isa 54:17)

This passage tells us why we don't have to be afraid. It's because as Christians, God protects us from the attacks and weapons of Satan. This passage tells us that "NO" weapon that Satan forms against us can prosper. The next part of the passage tells us exactly what the weapons represent. The weapons are "*the tongues that rise up against us.*"

Throughout this book we have discovered that our tongues can be used as a weapon. Whether it's a witch or sorcerer attempting to put a spell on us, or a person ignorantly using profanity attempting to evoke demon spirits to come upon us, they are all weapons.

The passage goes on to tell us that it's because of our heritage as servants of the Lord that we are protected. As a child of God, you walk under the canopy of God's protection (Psalm 91) from all witchcraft, spells, curses, and anything else anyone would attempt to put on you. You don't have to walk in fear, wondering if someone has put a spell on you. So do not walk in fear and paranoia, walk in faith, confidence and peace in Christ.

4. Cover Yourself

This passage (Isaiah 54:17) is a passage that we can use to help us walk in the faith and boldness of God. However, it is contingent upon the fact of whether or not you are *"properly"* covered. It takes two things for you to assure that you are properly covered. First, you must be born-again. Once again, the passage says that this protection applies to those who are *"servants"* or *"children"* of God. We become God's children through being born-again of God's Spirit. If you are not truly born-again, you have cause to be fearful, afraid and paranoid. Just as physical weapons are real and can cause death and destruction, the spiritual weapons can likewise do the same. But if you are truly born-again, you come under God's canopy of protection.

Psalms 91 is a good example of the divine protection that God gives us. This entire psalm should be confessed often. This psalm and other protective scriptures protect you against any and all of the weaponry and attacks of the devil.

The other thing that it takes to make sure that you are properly covered is the Word of God. In John, Chapter 3, a man by the name of Nichodemus asked Jesus what it took to become born-again. Jesus told him that in order to become born-again, he must be born of the water and the spirit. The spirit represents the Holy Spirit (being born-again), and the water represents the Word of God. It's through a combination of these two things that we become born-again. And, it's also through the combination of these two that we are protected. Being born-again of the Spirit of God is one part of it, but being covered in the Word of God is the other part of it.

Psalms 91 is a good scripture passage that you can use to cover your life, home and family. I encourage you to learn it by memory and confess it each day of your life. It covers everything from protection from dangers, sickness and disease, catastrophic dangers and many others.

In Ephesians 6:12 God instructs us to put on the whole armor of God. Part of clothing yourself in God's armor is to put on the protection of His Word. You need to begin a disciplined life of speaking the Word of God over your life and family each day. In Matthew 6:11, Jesus was teaching His disciples how to pray, through what we have come to know as *"The Lord's Prayer."* In this teaching, Jesus instructed them to ask for their *"daily bread."* We need to partake of our *"daily bread"* through praying and confessing God's Word each day. As we do so, we come under the complete hedge of God's protection.

When you are covered by God's Spirit and His Word, you can walk in complete peace and confidence. You can know (without a doubt) that no matter who speaks negative things about you, who attempts to put a curse upon you, or who speaks profanity witchcraft over you, that it will not prosper.

* Note: I encourage you to get our books entitled, *"The Weapons of our Warfare Volume 1 Prayers,* and *Vol. 3 Confessions."* These two books are filled with hundreds of scriptures on just about every area and concern of your life. Develop a pattern of prayer and confessions through these books. As you use them, you will begin to sense the anointing and power of God both in and upon your life.

5. Stop Using Profanity

You must stop using profanity immediately. I realize that for some, it is going to be difficult going cold turkey (stopping the use of profanity) when you have been using it your whole life, but you can do it.

First, you can do it because you now know what is actually going on in the spiritual realm. Knowing that you are calling upon demon spirits that brings destruction to your life and the lives of others when you use profanity should now be a great deterrent to using it.

Secondly, you can do it because of the power in Christ that is in you. Our Christian lives are filled with many different fleshly desires and temptations. But through the power and strength of Christ, we are able to resist and overcome them. The same way that we are able to resist and overcome other temptations of life is the same way you will be able to overcome this one. We do it with the anointing of God's spirit, the strength of the Holy Ghost, the power of God's Word, and a made up mind.

The third reason you must make a serious effort to stop using profanity is very important. In the previous point we discovered that when you have God's Spirit in you, and you properly cover yourself with the Word of

God, that no weapon (words or curses) that is formed against you shall prosper. This is absolutely true. However, this point is contingent upon whether or not you are actually opening the door for Satan.

When you use profanity, you are actually operating in witchcraft. In our previous chapters we have established that when a person operates in witchcraft, they are opening doors for demon spirits to come in and have access in their lives. So even though you are covering yourself with the Word of God (which closes the door to Satan to have access to your life), when you use profanity, you are opening the door right back up. So on one hand you are closing the front door to Satan, but on the other hand you are opening up the backdoor to him. This allows him to continue to have access to your life, and it allows the negative words, curses and profane words that others have spoken over you to now become effective and prosper against you (even though you are speaking the Word of God).

Make up in your heart and mind to close the front door and the back door by stopping the use of profanity.

6. Repent Again

If you do slip and fall to the temptation of using profanity, all is not lost. Like our other struggles in life, we do not give up if we fall. If you do succumb to the temptation to use profanity, repent quickly. Do not wait until your nightly prayer, repent immediately. Ask God to forgive you for what you have said. Ask Him to render the words you have spoken to be *null and void*; and ask Him to strengthen you and keep you from falling and doing it again.

Do this each and every time you fall to the use of profanity. If you have to do it twenty times a day, then do it. If you find yourself slipping back into a habitual pattern of using profanity again, pray the repentance prayer again. You might even want to read the book over again in order to get your soul sober concerning what is happening in the spiritual realm.

When I first began trying to erase profanity from my life, I used it on average of three or four times a day. Shortly afterwards, I was down to only once or twice a week. Before I knew it, it was only once or twice a year. And, soon it was completely gone. Each time I fell to it, I would repent immediately and ask for God's help and deliverance. Each time I prayed this short prayer, the Lord would help me more and more until it was completely gone.

You can and will be set free from the use of profanity. With the knowledge of what you have been doing, along with continual repentance, prayer, the confession of God's Word, and a made up mind, your use of profanity will practically vanish from your vocabulary in no time.

7. Reject Satan's Deception

Be not deceived: evil communications corrupt good manners. (Cor 15:33)

The above passage is giving us a warning that we should "not" be deceived by Satan. The paraphrased version of this passage says that *evil language [profanity] will bring corruption to a godly lifestyle.* Don't let Satan deceive you. If he hasn't already done it, he will begin telling you that what you have read in this book is just a bunch of rhetoric and nonsense. As you desire to turn your life away from the use of profanity, he will continue to insist that there is nothing wrong with you using profanity. The reason why he is telling you this is because he wants to continue to have demonic access to your life by keeping you blinded from the truth.

The truth is that profanity is a weapon of Satan. It is just as real of a weapon as a knife or gun. He has been using it to hinder your life, your family's lives, and even the lives of your children. To continue his rampage of destruction he is counting on two things—ignorance and deception. Now that you know the truth about profanity and witchcraft, he can no longer use ignorance. And, if your spirit is open to receive the truth, he can no longer use deception.

Reject Satan's attempt to continue to deceive you, and receive God's truth about profanity. As you change your life and stop the use of profanity, you will cut off Satan's access to your life. You will also open the spiritual channels to receive the blessings God has ordained for you.

Repentance Prayer for Profanity

Father, I come boldly before You in the name of Jesus Christ asking that You would forgive me for practicing the doctrine of Balaam through the use of profanity.

I want to thank You for giving me spiritual knowledge and understanding concerning profanity, and not allowing me to live the rest of my life using it in ignorance as I have done thus far. Thank You for revealing the spirit of truth unto me.

Now that I know the truth concerning profanity, I now confess and acknowledge my ways and the sinful deeds of my mouth before You. I'm asking that You would forgive me for every word of profanity that I've spoken.

Forgive me for practicing the Doctrine of Balaam through the words of my mouth. Forgive me for practicing witchcraft—which I've done through speaking idle, vain and profane words. And, forgive me for causing hindrances, as well as physical and spiritual harm to others through my use of profanity.

I now denounce Satan and every demon and devil that I have ever called upon through my words and the use of profanity. I denounce their power, influence and presence over my life and the lives of others I've spoken over. I now cut off their power and presence; I break every curse, and I render every evil spirit that has ever been established over my life and the lives of others through my profane words to be helpless, powerless, inoperative and ineffective. I decree all these things by the power, blood and the mighty name of the Lord, Jesus Christ.

Father, for every place I have ever released the presence of evil and demonic spirits through the use of negative words, curses and profanity, I now ask that you would release the peace of your spirit. For every person's life that I have ever cursed or caused harm through vain words, curses and profanity, I now pray for Your presence to be over their lives instead; and I now pray for a hundred-fold blessing from You Father to now be released over their lives, family lives, and their surroundings and circumstances.

I'm asking that You would now sanctify my heart, mind and soul from profanity and the use of it. And, may you create within me a clean heart, and renew a right spirit within me.

Father, Your Word says that You are able to keep us from falling. I pray therefore that when anger attempts to rise upon me and I am tempted to use profanity, that You would keep me from sinning. Keep me from the evil of my tongue and the use of profanity. Set a watch (of the Holy Spirit) over my mouth, and by Your power and strength, may You keep the doors of my lips. And, may You cause the words of my mouth and the meditation of my heart to be acceptable in Your sight.

Father, You said in Your Word that You have set before us life and death, blessings and cursings. Help me to no longer use my mouth as an instrument of unrighteousness unto sin by speaking death and curses. But help me from this day forth instead, to use my mouth as an instrument of righteousness by speaking life and blessings over my life and over the lives of others around me.

In the name of the Lord, Jesus Christ, I pray. AMEN

Warfare Cleansing Prayer

Father, I come boldly before You in the name of Jesus Christ asking You to cleanse my heart and spirit from the heaviness of this movie (or atmosphere).

Father, in Your Word You have declared that no weapon that is formed against us shall be able to prosper. You have also declared that every evil word that is spoken over, about, or against us shall fall to the ground. So by the authority of Your Word, I declare that no weapons of negative words, curses, or profanity that has been spoken over my life (or in the atmosphere of this movie), shall be able to prosper against me or my life in any way. I also declare that every evil word that has been directed towards my life shall fall to the ground.

Your Word tells us to cast off every work of darkness and put on the armor of light. So by the authority and power of Your Word, I bind and I loose every evil spirit, influence, and power of darkness that has attempted to rest upon me as a result of this movie *(or being in this atmosphere)*. I loose every stronghold and every evil spirit that would attempt to cling to my life. I loose their ability to cling to my spirit or soul; and I cast them off of my soul, heart and spirit by the authority of God in the name of Jesus Christ.

Father, I thank You for the hedge of Your spirit by the anointing. I'm asking that You would now cover my life with the anointing. For Your Word has declared that the anointing breaks and destroys every yoke and stronghold of the devil. Because of the power of Your Word and Your anointing upon my life, I decree every curse, and every word of profanity, and every evil spirit to be helpless, powerless, inoperative and ineffective to prosper against my life, my home or my surroundings in any way.

Now Father, I'm asking that You would purge my heart, mind and spirit from the spiritually dangerous effects of this movie. May You also sanctify and cleanse my heart, and renew a right and godly spirit within me.

Father, You gave us the authority in Your Word to release Your presence and peace upon a situation. Therefore I release this spirit of heaviness from my life, and I release Your presence and Spirit of peace to be over my life and upon my heart and soul instead. And, I shall therefore walk and rest in your peace — the peace that surpasses all understanding.

I decree all these things by the power, blood, and the invincible name of the Lord, Jesus Christ! AMEN.

I call heaven and earth to record this day against you, that I have set before you life and death, blessing and cursing: therefore choose life, that both thou and thy seed may live.

Deu 30:1

Death and life are in the power of the tongue: and they that love it shall eat the fruit thereof.

Prov 18:21

Other Books By Kenneth Scott

The Weapons Of Our Warfare, Volume 1
This is a handbook of scriptural based prayers for just about every need in your life. There are prayers for your home, marriage, family and many personal issues that we face in our lives each day. If you desire to be developed in prayer, then this is a must book for you.

The Weapons Of Our Warfare, Volume 2
It is a sequel of Volume I, and brings the prayer warrior into the ministry of intercession. It has prayers for your church, pastor, city, our nation, and many other national issues in which we should pray for. If you desire to be developed as an intercessor, then this book is for you.

The Weapons Of Our Warfare, Volume 3
(Confessing God's Word Over Your Life)
There is a difference between prayer and confession. This book gives the believer understanding about confessions and what they do in your life. It also contains daily confessions for major areas of your life. If you have Volumes 1 & 2, then you also need Volume 3.

The Weapons Of Our Warfare Volumes 1 ,2 & 3 on CD
Meditate on the Word of God as it is prayed on audio CDs. These CDs contain prayers from Volumes 1 2, & 3 (sold separately). As you hear these prayers prayed, you can stand in the spirit of agreement and apply them in the spirit to your life, situations and circumstances as you ride in your car, or as you sit in your home.

The Weapons Of Our Warfare, Volume 4
(Prayers for Teens and Young Adults)
Teenagers have different needs than adults. This is a prayer handbook that keeps the same fervency and fire as Volumes 1 & 2, but also addresses the needs of teens. This book is a "must" for your teens.

The Weapons Of Our Warfare, Volume 5, "The Warfare of Worship"
Through the warfare of "praise and worship," this book teaches you how to go on the assault against the forces of darkness and tear Satan's kingdom down in your life and circumstances. Psalm 68:1 tells us that when God arises, the enemy becomes scattered. When you praise, you raise! In other words, when you praise and Worship God, He begins to rise up on you, in you, in your presence, your surroundings, and even in your situations and circumstances. Since the enemy cannot stand God's presence, he has to scatter and flee, releasing and leaving your stuff behind.

The Weapons of our Warfare, Vol 6, "Decreeing Your Healing"
This book contains 160 spiritual warfare healing declarations that will help you decree and declare your healing. It also contains vital principles and precepts that will help you to understand that you have a blood bought right (by Christ) to be healed. Get this book and learn how to "take by force" your healing through the authority of God's Word.

Praying in Your Divine Authority
Many Christians are hindered and defeated by Satan simply because they do not know the dominion and authority they have in Christ. This book teaches the believer how to bind and loose Satan and demon spirits, and how to pray and walk in our divine authority.

When All Hell Breaks Loose
Most mature Christians can survive a casual trial here and there, but many of God's people fall during the storms of life. Get this book and learn how to prevail through the storm *"When all Hell Breaks Loose."*

The Warfare of Fasting
Jesus said that some spiritual strongholds, hindrances and bondages will only be broken through prayer and fasting. This book teaches the believer the different types of fasts, the methods of fasting, and the warfare of what happens in the spiritual realm when we fast. If you want to see "total" deliverance in your life, you need to get this book.

Standing In The Gap
In this book Pastor Scott teaches life-changing principles of what it means to make up the hedge, stand in the gap, stand in agreement, and intercede for others. If you are a prayer warrior, an intercessor, or you have a desire to be one, this book is a "must" for you.

Too Blessed To Be Cursed
Do generational curses actually exist? Where do they come from? Does God send generational curses upon my life, or are they from the devil? Could it be that some of my difficulties and struggles in life come from generational curses? If there is a curse on my life or family, can it be broken? Using the life of David, Pastor Scott answers these and other questions about generational curses and teaches how we become set free and break them through the power of the blood of Jesus Christ. There is also a chapter of decrees and declarations for you to take and speak and break these chains of curses and hindrances in your life and family line through the blood of Jesus Christ.

The Basics of Prayer — Understanding The Lord's Prayer
Just about all of us have prayed "The Lord's Prayer," and even know The Lord's Prayer by memory. But very few of us really understand the depths of what Jesus was truly teaching His disciples in this prayer outline. This book gives the believer a scripture by scripture breakdown of this prayer and gives illumination and insight on its understanding.

Why We Act Like That!
Pastor Scott traces the root cause of many African American issues of today to the spirit of slavery. He parallels the problems the Children of Israel had with post Egyptian bondage to issues African Americans now face in the post slavery era. He shows us that it's a slavery mindset that is still influencing many of the issues that African Americans deal with to this very day. He also shows us how we can overcome them through the power of God, His Word, and deliverance.

Contact Us:

For questions or comments, write to:

Spiritual Warfare Ministries
Attention: Kenneth Scott
P.O. Box 2024
Birmingham, Alabama 35201-2024

(205) 853-9509

Web Site: www.prayerwarfare.com
Or
Spiritualwarfare.cc

email us at prayerbooks@aol.com

This book is not available in all bookstores. To order additional copies of this book, please visit our website. You may also order by mail by sending $11.99 plus $2.98 shipping and handling to the above address.

Made in the USA
Columbia, SC
18 July 2023